the family portrait

A JOURNEY OF HOPE THROUGH THE EYES OF THE FATHERLESS

TIM FROST

Jenny, thank you so much! Always
so inspiring to see your beautiful
photos!

†im

dedicated to my wife, son,
and daughter for forever changing
the meaning of family for me

CONTENTS

FOREWORD

This book was originally written for my own personal healing and it has become so much more. We believe that in uncovering the darkness of our past, shame slowly disappears and it is replaced with a light. That light can then spread to others.

My story will reveal difficult moments of sexual and physical abuse, drug abuse and trauma. In those moments, I hope not that you feel pity toward me, or anger toward my abusers. I have forgiven my mother and I love her deeply. She did the best she could with all of us boys and has struggled in her own life with many of the happenings that also plagued me. I hope rather you can read these pages and they can inspire you to share your heartaches with a loved one, to learn to forgive so it doesn't continue to poison your well, and mostly to simply love yourself and others more.

Notes:

Some names have been changed to respect identity.

**Within these pages you will notice segments that quickly shift to moments of "now" without explanation. I placed these throughout to show what my life looks now juxtaposed to the darkest days of my existence. There is hope. Always.*

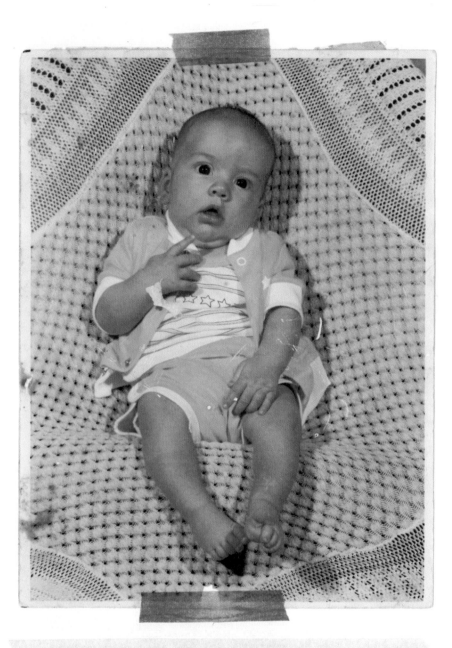

me before my first memory

CHAPTER ONE
The Trailer

before innocence was lost

That house was cold and dark. Most of the time it was because we either forgot to pay the gas and electric, or Mom spent the money on alcohol and drugs. (oops) I have a lot of memories from that house. Some good, most sad and bleak. There was always an evil tinge to the air, most likely from Mom belonging to a Satanic cult the entire time we lived there. She was always doing weird séances and rituals, but I'll get to that later.

I guess the only way to start off is to go back to the beginning, to my first memory…

First Memory

I was two years old. It was a winter night. I'm not sure what month it was, but I do remember having on my zip-up pajamas with the built-in padded feet. My three brothers were already sound asleep in the add-on part of our trailer that Grandpa had built. I was too scared to sleep out there, so I always slept in Mom's room. That night she had been drinking her special juice that only moms were allowed to drink—and lots of it. I was getting ready to climb into bed and hear a bedtime story, or hopefully fall asleep to an episode of Chips, that old motorcycle cop show.

All of a sudden, Mom came out of the bathroom. She was coming toward me, crying and telling me to get against the wall. I was so scared; I did what she said.

Without hesitation, she pulled a black metal pole with a wooden handle and a trigger from under the covers. She pointed it straight at my face from about six feet away.

"I love you. I'm sorry."

The next thing I heard was the loudest, most earth-shattering noise my ears have ever experienced. Then silence.

The whole world slowed down to a mere photograph snapped in time. After a few seconds (which seemed like hours), I heard a ringing, the loudest ringing you can possibly imagine. And just barely over that ringing, I could hear a most mournful cry as she scooped me up and squeezed out what little air I had left. She kept saying, "I'm sorry. I'm so sorry."

As I was in my mother's embrace, I turned to look at the wall where once I had been sitting. There was a hole about the same size as my head in the exact position where my head had been. The hole made a clean break through the fake wood panel wall of the trailer and went all the way through to the bathroom on the other side.

At that time, I was absolutely oblivious to the magnitude of what had just happened. I think I was in a form of shock because I had never seen or heard anything like that before. I didn't even know what had happened or that Mom had done it. For all I knew there was some sort of creature who had made that deafening sound and gaping hole. Mom seemed to be in a state of shock too, mostly because she knew there was no way that shot could have missed my head unless Something Divine had taken place.

But why would Someone or Something out there have an inkling of me, a thought to save me from this fate?

It was obvious, but I didn't know it then. My life had a bigger purpose than the mess in which I was raised.

A plan was already made that I had yet to fulfill.

New Normal

A young boy awakens in his bed, custom-designed to match the pallet wood wall his dad built, swallowing the room with comfort and warmth. A father slowly brings the room alive with light as he pulls back the curtains—morning sun pushes through. Silently he gathers clothes from the closet, grabs the young boys' shoes and places them on the bed as the boy opens his heavy eyelids again to a new day. The boy is then greeted with a gentle hug and a kiss from his mother as she brings today's pre-breakfast to him in true hobbit form. The mom and dad work as a team dressing the teenage boy who cannot speak or have the ability to dress himself on his own. Although the interaction between the three is usually made with little to no words; everyone is able to communicate exactly what they want to get across. This morning routine has become the heartbeat that begins most of our days.

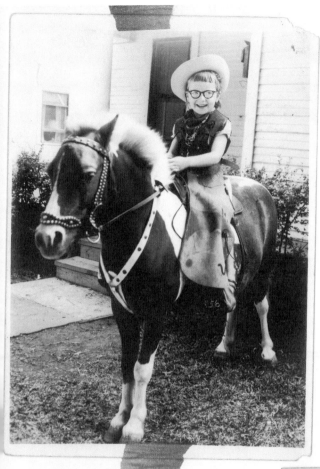

my mom

Duck ride
Age 2

Pony ride 1955

probably playing the beatles

9

An Unknown Language

So I guess you could say that there was a lot of weird stuff going on in the trailer. The funny thing is, at the time it didn't seem weird to me at all. I actually didn't understand the complexity of the things that were going on until much later. Yes, I was scared a lot, but what kid isn't scared all the time?

One thing that scared me the most was Mom's weird friends.

They would come over at all times of the day and night, wearing black, silky clothes. Everything about them was dark, from their broomstick-stiff matted hair to their polished black boots. With skin as white as sidewalk chalk, they looked as if they had been hidden in a cave on the darkest part of the moon.

Due to a strange, fearful feeling they gave me, I never really said anything to them, but I knew if they were Mom's friends they had to be ok. Mom would never let bad guys come over, right?

As soon as all her friends were there, they would lock themselves in a musty back room used mainly for storage space. I was never invited to play the games they played together, but I snuck in a few times and watched with sheer amazement at the way they were acting. Most of the time I had to keep from laughing because it sounded so ridiculous.

There were four people sitting directly across from each other in a circle. There was Mom, a lady who was a bit smaller with squinty eyes, and two men, both tall and skinny. Each of the men had a tiny bit of hair just on the bottom of his chin, which was funny looking in itself. In the middle of the circle, they had laid a black blanket with an off-white star painted upon it. The star seemed to have a face and horns, kind of the like the goats at the zoo. One eye was visible while the other eye seemed to have a deep crimson stain covering not only it, but a part of where the nose of the goat should've been as well. Then they would take candles and each would light one, saying, "Wind. Earth. Sky. Body." After that they began to speak in a made-up language that sounded like a rooster pen and Porky Pig mixed together.

I had to thrust my entire face into one of the pillows on the floor to keep from being exposed, I was laughing so hard. The feeling of hilarity was soon broken by a swarm of black shadows instantly filling the room after the chant was over. Too scared to run and too frozen to scream, the only comfort I had was to take the pillow, cover my face and think of a different place. My brain was working so hard to keep the thought of what I had seen out and all my good thoughts in that I soon fell asleep. I awoke to find Mom looking me over with the disgust in her eyes that she usually reserved for when I had done something really bad.

my typical look of curiosity

"How long have you been lying there?" she asked. "You shouldn't have been in here! Why do you have to be so nosy? Go to bed now!"

I did as she said, fast as my little legs could move. It was way past dark now. Everyone else was in bed and Mom's friends had gone. After a few minutes of lying alone in the big bed in Mom's room, she came in and acted as if nothing had happened. She cuddled me and we both started to fall asleep. The last thought I remember having was, what did I do wrong...and why was Mom so upset?

The Men

"Are you my Dad?"

That seemed to be a common question I had in my head every time I saw Mom with a guy at the house. Most of the time I was too afraid to even give the men a second look for fear that their gaze might pierce my insides like a harpoon. These weren't your everyday, go-to-the-office-job guys. They were usually rough looking, smelling of fermented fruit and cigarette smoke.

My least favorite thing about when the men came over was how they kept Mom from me for hours. They would lock her in her room, and the sounds that came out of there were terrifying. It sounded as if a small tornado was thrashing and throwing everything across the room while Mom screamed to the top of her lungs. Most of the time I was just ignored while I cried and begged for them to stop and let Mom out, but sometimes the men would tell me to shut up, using words I only knew from watching the action movies with my brothers that we weren't supposed to watch. Often I just ended up falling asleep outside the bedroom door. The men would be gone by the time I awoke.

I would ask Mom why she let them come over and tell her how much I hated it when they were there. After months of her not answering, she finally got mad at me and said, "Don't you want me to be happy? Do you not like eating? Do you even know what those men do for me?"

The only reaction I knew was just to be quiet and not say a word to that. I didn't know why Mom had bursts of anger sometimes, but I guess she didn't either. She apologized and told me it wasn't my fault.

"I'm just taking out frustration."

As confusing as it was then, I just took it in stride and let it be. The embrace felt good enough to soothe my worries. The men were gone, and even though I knew they would be back, it was ok for now.

brother

older brother

oldest brother

brother's birthday

Christmas 1989-ish

me and a cannon ???

3 months after christmas
still exicited about the tree

older brother's piano
recital 1980-something

The Buffet Trick

Free food.

Free anything.

Always a good thing in our house. Growing up with three brothers and only one parent's income, you had to have tricks for survival. One of our favorites was The Buffet Trick.

There was a restaurant down the street by the lake that we would go to every few weeks. We would pile inside the old, rust-colored Chevy Nova. Usually Mom would have to bang the battery with a rock a few times before it would start, and when it finally did, it put off the most putrid smoke from underneath. It looked like we made up half of the supply of clouds in the sky during thunderstorms...you know, the dark, eerie ones.

We were assigned positions on the way there, kind of like agents in an old spy movie. Mom would call out different foods and tell us who was going to get what. One day I got chicken fried steak. One brother got mashed potatoes, another corn. Oldest was assigned to rolls.

When we got to the restaurant, we all put on our backpacks that Mom had lined with plastic wrap from the grocery store. We all went through the buffet line, and I grabbed as many chicken fried steaks as I could fit on my plate. There was an older man next to me. "Big appetite for such a small tyke." I just nodded and smiled, then went back to the table in the corner.

We all took turns on lookout to see if anyone was coming as we piled our assigned foods into the backpacks. Mine was so heavy that I had to switch out with the rolls backpack. After all the packs were filled to the brim, we hid them under the table, then ate like kings. The food might not have been the greatest, but we would never have known. This was luxury food.

The best part of this feast was that it was Wednesday, and kids ate free on Wednesdays. So for five dollars, we definitely got our money's worth. It was kind of like grocery shopping except much more fun, and the food was way better than anything Mom could ever cook. We stuffed our faces until we thought we would explode if we ate one more bite, then took our backpacks filled with dinner for at least the next week and drove home. Mom gave us a thumbs up and said, "Mission successful!"

Not only did it feel good to have full bellies, but also to do something right that made Mom happy. Sometimes she was hard to please, but every time we did The Buffet Trick, things were good.

Saw Something I Can't Explain

So, you know when you're a kid and you get scared at night, thinking there is some sort of foul, three-headed, fire-eating, wart-bearing monster in your closet? Well, I just wished that was real. The things I saw at night were far more dark and terrifying.

The first time it happened, Mom and I were sitting on our dirt brown secondhand couch. I think it used to be more of a light sand color, but with four dirty boys who bathed about once a week and clumsily spilt alcohol on worn cushions, you can imagine how it looked now. We were watching Rambo on the foil-wrapped black and white TV. The picture wasn't that great, but it didn't matter. Anything could have been showing on that screen and I would have been glued to it like bugs to a light bulb. Even though the picture wasn't very good, the sound was immaculate. The plastic knob was broken, so there was only one volume—piercing. For me it was almost unbearable when watching the news or other boring shows, but when action movies or cartoons played, it was like a sweet lullaby.

Mom had just sent everyone else to bed because getting them up for school on eight hours of sleep was a chore in itself. She said I could stay and watch until the next commercial. I didn't last five more minutes. The sound of the gunshots and explosions vibrated off my ears, and I was soon fast asleep. However, the euphoria soon died out.

I awoke to a very dark, uninviting living room. My body felt as if I had been sleeping on the cold, rocky floor outside. Then I felt the presence of someone or something skew into my gaze. I looked to see Mom standing over the couch, but as I said her name, a deep black shadow swooped over and engulfed her face. It flew through each corner of our house like a cloud of smoke. I screamed to the top of my lungs and ran down the narrow hallway into her room.

She was there, lying in bed with both eyes open, yet not awake. I pounded repeatedly on her chest to wake her, but to no avail. Whether it was due to my tiny arms and puny strength or to her almost coma-like trance, I don't know, but she didn't budge.

Finally, after all my strength gave out and all my tears were poured, she awoke as if from taking a light snooze. She saw that I was in distress, and the first thing she said to me was, "Did you see it? It's ok if you did."

The reassurance that she knew what was going on without me even telling her was more than enough for me then. Yet as time went on and I saw the figures more and more, it never seemed ok. It was always something terrible...dark...unknown. It was something I could not explain.

The Cemetery

The cemetery was only a few feet from the fence that lined our property. There was a McDonald's inside the covered area used for funerals on rainy days. I had never actually been there, but my brothers told me all about it. They said I was too young to go, because you had to be a certain height to reach the entrance. Then one day they made an exception.

After a year of wanting and wishing, I was finally going to get my way. We would have to wait until it was completely dark so that my age and height could be concealed by the night. As soon as the sky was covered in black and Mom had put us all down for the night, we made our way out of the back door and toward the strip of woods separating the cemetery from our house. There was a barbed wire fence that we carefully maneuvered through, making sure none of the metal shards seared our clothes or skin. We were now on the home stretch to the pavilion. With the comfort of my brothers there, the cemetery seemed much less scary than I had imagined. Usually I was not allowed to do anything that they did, so this was an exceptionally unordinary day for me. I was feeling pumped.

When we got inside the covering without walls, my brothers showed me the opening in the ceiling that led to the McDonald's I had been anticipating for so long. I was hoisted on Oldest Brother's shoulders and lifted gently into the opening, probably seven feet off the ground. I used what little strength I had to pull myself the rest of the way inside; what I saw and heard then made me so angry at myself! I knew I should have expected as much, but that hope inside had made me ignore my natural instinct of staying in bed. I could hear laughing and the sound of feet rustling through leaves at a running pace.

"Bring me back a happy meal!" they taunted as I sat there, stuck in the attic of an empty building with absolutely no sign of life anywhere.

I had been fooled again.

I scrambled for the opening and hung from it, trying to get down, but I was still a good way from the concrete floor. The strength in my tiny arms failed me as I fell flat on the bottom bones of my back. I knew crying would not get me out of this scary place any faster, so I managed to pick myself up and run in the direction of home, only letting out a few teardrops.

Not only did my strength fail me, but my memory did as well as I came upon the barbed fence. It grabbed my legs right above the knees and the momentum spun

forever gullible... and a little sassy

me into a face-forward somersault over the rest of the fence.

Legs and head bleeding, back swelling and bruised, I finally made it back home, only to get yelled at by Mom. I tried to explain what happened, but was cut short with questions.

"Why do you always have to be the one to get into stuff? Why can't you be more like your brothers and go to sleep when you are told? You are worthless. I don't have time to play nurse with you now. I have to go to work!"

I went straight to bed, my brothers laughing and mocking me all the while. I vowed that next time: I would be smarter. My gullible insides knew better now—or at least until next time.

Captain, My Captain

One of the things I was really good at was using my imagination. Sometimes too good, even to the point that I actually believed cartoons were real. I would think that I had a little Care Bear blood in me.

On this summer day, I was inside the ceramic shop. It was an old white barn converted into a place to pour, set and fire ceramics. There were over a million molds of all kinds, hidden in every nook where things could be shoved. There were houses to make a city with ice rinks, churches, and even igloos; cups with Santa faces and plates with kitten decals; farm animals and Baby Jesuses. You could find anything you wanted there.

The layout was a maze in itself. When you first walked in, you would see completed works on all the shelves, glossy and fragile, for inspiration or purchase. Then around the other side were four tables where ladies would sit all day, painting or scraping their molds.

In the next room were the kilns. When they were on, you could barely be in the room for more than a few minutes without your skin burning and feeling the need to pass out.

The back was my favorite part; it was where the hundreds...no, thousands of molds were hidden. There were passageways and cave-like entrances at every turn that seemed to go on for miles. That is where I spent most of my time in the shop.

On this particular day, I was on a mission to climb to the top of the highest shelf to get a stolen treasure back from pirates who had hidden it there. I was the captain and Grandpa was my co-captain, so he was off on the other side of the shelves pouring mud for the journey back home. I had started my climb to the top, when I suddenly heard a yell from the co-captain. As I grabbed onto the second tier of shelving, it started to break with a creaking sound that could have been heard on the moon. It sounded like a tree falling. I lost my grasp and landed on the dirt floor with a thud that knocked out my breath. I looked up to see a massive mold from the broken shelf come tumbling down toward me. I closed my eyes and tightened my body for the impact, but the next thing I felt wasn't the mold at all—it was a foot shoving me with such force that I rolled ten feet from where I had lain. I heard an unbearable yell coming from my co-captain. The mold had landed on his leg; all I saw was blood and a bone protruding from the skin by his kneecap. He yelled for me to get Granny, so I ran, fast as lightning.

this ceramic shop was a castle of
my imagination. Anything was possible

Grandpa, my Co-captain

When she got there, I tried to explain about the pirates and the treasure and the climb, but was immediately silenced. All he said was that a mold fell on him. He never blamed me for this accident or told anyone I had a part in it. I have always thought that I failed him as a captain—it should have been him who was in charge instead of me.

The Bear

That night something came to our house that I only know as the Bear.

We had just finished an episode of The Twilight Zone, to which I had fallen in and out of sleep. (This was a very strange show that always made me feel weird or scared after it was over, so most often I would try not to finish it.) Instead of waking up to the sound of Mom clicking off the TV, I awoke to a much more intense, almost gnawing sound. I could hear Mom screaming and a commotion coming from the living room, so I started for the bedroom door but was immediately stopped. Grandpa was at the door with an axe and yelled for me to stay in the room and DO NOT COME OUT for anything. I was even more scared now, wondering if I was having one of my weird Twilight Zone nightmares. Was this really happening?

I darted under the covers and closed my eyes as hard as I could, trying to wake myself or start dreaming of more pleasant things. I heard Grandpa yell, "Get outta here, Bear! Stay away from my daughter and my family and NEVER step foot on my property again."

A bear?? That's why Grandpa had his axe—there was a bear trying to get into our house and eat us just like in the cartoons I had seen! I felt a sensation come over me that I had never felt before...pride. I felt like Grandpa was King of the Universe, Protector of all the Trailer Kingdom. I heard a slamming and breaking of what sounded like the entire kitchen, then after a few moments, the squealing of tires and more yelling. A bear driving away in a car? Yes, this was a dream.

The next thing I knew, the sun was coming through the window by the bed and I could hear clamoring in the kitchen. Mom was sweeping up piles and piles of dishes; it looked like someone had opened a puzzle box of glass on the floor. Grandpa was putting yellow wooden slats over holes in the wall that definitely were not there when I had fallen asleep the night before. My eyes widened like the windows on this sunny day, and immediately I asked with enthusiasm, "Grandpa, did you slay a bear last night?"

He and Mom exchanged glances. He simply said, "You will never have to worry about bears again."

He smiled and I knew he was the hero in this story.

my pet monster, me, & the "babysitter"

The Babysitter

There was one thing I enjoyed more than anything else as a kid. It was the babysitter—a thirteen-inch, black and white, Magnavox television with dust encrusted in every crack it could find.

It was the source of most of my world knowledge at the time, whether it came from discovering different cartoon sounds, hearing about the Korean War through Hawkeye and Klinger, or learning about alcohol with Sam and Norm.

The babysitter was my comfort, and I knew everything about him. When he got fuzzy, I'd dress him in aluminum. When he wouldn't come on, I'd pat gently on his back. I even learned to find a metal object around the house, whether it was a hanger, a paperclip or a rusted safety pin, and attach it to his back to help him come through to me more clearly. Too many hours of my life to count, he was there.

One of the few things I actually felt in control of.

The Kidnappers

With Oldest Brother sick and Next Down visiting his dad, I got to be the puppy on a leash for Other Brother's fulfillment. Following him around, I did every trick and flew through any hoop he threw toward me. It was not rewarding in any aspect except that I got to feel accepted by someone who normally despised every tiny detail about me. It wouldn't last long, so I knew I had to hang onto every moment and follow every command like a trained Navy Seal.

We (and when I say "we", I mean "he") decided to go to the graveyard and color in the carved names on the ancient graves. The crevices seemed to pick up the wax from the crayons like our shoes picked up dirt on a rainy day. The feeling of the granite vibrating as we carved away in every color of the rainbow was almost as satisfying as the actual end result.

This went on for about an hour. Then we would jump from one grave to another, pretending that if we missed and hit the grass, we would be sucked into an under-world with man-eating dogs and two-headed horses with horns. (We would take special care not to miss.)

While we were jumping, an old, dirty, brown van with rust stains around the bottom exterior pulled up in the graveyard driveway. I had just learned a lot of my letters and recognized a capital R A M on the side below the door. A man with eyes as black as night rolled the foggy, smoke-stained window down on the passenger side and asked if we knew how to get to the ceramic shop. We both started talking immediately, excited that we knew the answer to an adult's question. Of course, I was quickly silenced by Brother's dominance over me; then he started again to tell him. The man stopped him and motioned us to come closer, that he couldn't hear what we were saying.

Out of the corner of my eye, I saw the back door open and a short, stumpy, little man jumped out with such force that he ended up tripping and landing on his patchy bearded face. The sound and motion startled me to the point where I let out a scream that could've broken glass. We both began to run toward the woods that marked the property line between the house and the cemetery. I could hear yelling after us.

"Get them! Those are her kids!"

Our knowledge of the shortcuts and secret passages home worked to our advantage, and we were back at the ceramic shop before the men even had time to get back to their van. We started speaking ninety miles a minute to Granny about what had happened, and she went straight to the phone to dial the police. With us living ten miles in any direction of a town, it took a while for anyone to show up. When they did, the van had moved on from its failed mission.

How they knew who we were and why they wanted us remained a mystery for more than half of my life.

Snakes on a Plain

Clumsy.

Accident prone.

Misfortunate.

Call it what you will, but I call it being me. If there was a one in a million chance of something bad happening to someone, I would place all the chips on myself.

In the July of my fourth year of life, we had started a game of Capture the Flag with all my brothers and cousins. Capture the Flag is a game in which there are two teams, with one person guarding the color flag of their team while everyone else sneaks around and tries to steal it. The way we played, if you were seen, you would get rotten pears fallen from our tree thrown at you, and when hit, you would have to sit in the isolation tank for five minutes. (As if rotten pear all over you wasn't punishment enough.) The tank was really an aluminum cow trough that we turned upside down and made into our prison. It was not the most pleasant smell or feeling, being inside this tank.

In this particular game, I was advancing on the north side of the house with dirty, bare feet, sneaking on the tips of my toes. I was trying to be as stealthy as I could, breathing slowly as if I were contemplating deep sleep...and then there it was. Walking in a yard so dark that I could only see by the light that the stars were putting out, I stepped on a large stick. This didn't feel like any other stick though. It was almost leathery and ridged, like old, refrigerated hamburger meat. I then felt one of the sharpest pains of my life—like someone had taken a fork and stabbed it directly into the left side of my foot. I screamed as the pain took over, then ran as far as I could before collapsing in front of the rundown porch.

Brother was the one guarding the flag and it startled him to the point of almost falling off the porch. The game was immediately put on hold as they all came to my side to assess the commotion. They took one look at my foot and knew what had happened. I was still oblivious; all I knew was that my foot felt like it had been doused in gasoline and lit ablaze.

I was lifted into a wheelbarrow and wheeled down to the shop where Grandpa was doing some late-night ceramic firing for a customer that would be there the next day. He stopped dead in his work, grabbed the keys to the old Lincoln and started driving as fast as people do when they are heading for the moon.

Within what felt like a few minutes, I was in a very white place with very long halls and doors at every corner. Finally, we stopped in a room about the size of a small bathroom. They started poking and mashing on the foot, now swollen to almost the same size as Grandpa's feet. I remember hearing the words "copperhead", "poison", "snakebite", and "venom", just seconds before a needle the size of the Sears Tower was stabbed into me. After that there were tears and drowsiness and a couple bags of ice trying to freeze my foot off.

It seemed as if I was in there all night, but I was later told that it only took them about an hour to get the swelling to go down. I went home, lying on the couch-sized backseat, weaving in and out of my dreams.

For the next six months, I was not able to walk around or do anything for myself. I did learn how to crawl like a crab to get to the major destinations—bathroom, couch, TV. Also, I was told that my six months was the same as two weeks in regular human time.

Time can be a tricky thing when you're a kid.

this skate-scoot was so rad

pure childlike wonder

It Never Happened

It never happened.

It never happened.

It didn't.

No matter how much I say that to myself, it never fills the hole dug deep like a coal miner's cave inside my chest.

Then the question why. Why did it happen? As I fill that hole to the top with more questions than answers, my thoughts eventually go back to that night. Those nights.

Mom had a boyfriend that was part of her cult. We would stay with him probably two or three nights a week. He was a tall, skinny man with balding, baseball cap hair and coffee stained teeth. The kind of man you would see scratching lotto tickets at your local gas station with a beer in hand. He had a voice that was in the same vein as a rabid dog trying to bark with a sinus infection. You could barely understand anything he said, and when it was audible, it was usually something really rude and degrading. Needless to say, he was not favored by myself or anyone I knew, except Mom. I hoped and wished the nights we had to stay at his house would be few and far between, but they always seemed to come again as soon as they had ended. My brothers were at my cousin's house the first time it happened...

Mom drank her sauce and smoked her special cigarettes all through the night, while I was fed a mayonnaise and bread sandwich. The flavor was similar to Elmer's glue and cardboard mixed together on cabinets covered with ashtrays. The more Quitman tap water I drank, the less I had to endure the taste. When Mom had enjoyed all she could take, she usually passed out on the couch, not to be woken up at any decent hour before noon the next day. As I was lying down to fall asleep, her boyfriend grabbed me hard enough to leave red marks on my tiny wrists and took me forcefully to the dirt red barn behind the house.

There were lots of different animals sleeping inside, including pigs, cows, rabbits and chickens. In the corner, there was a brown dog about half the size of me, limping to the blanket that laid near the pig sty. I was told to take off all my clothes by that raspy, hateful voice. I did as I was told for fear of being hurt, knowing Mom was fast asleep and any resistance would only make things worse. I was forced to hold the poor animal that had limped to the blanket by the head while this man got behind it and forced himself on her. I wasn't sure what was happening, but I knew the dog was in pain. The sounds I heard made me want to run and wake someone to help me keep this from happening, but I was frozen. The next few minutes slowly swept by like a never-ending dream. I remember the warm tears just started streaming out like a river in the summer.

After everything was over, I opened my eyes to the man rubbing on my shoulders, hands almost grasping my neck. He had been yelling at me with that sick voice, calling me names that I didn't know what they meant, but I knew they were hateful because they were the same words he yelled at the TV when sports were on. "You dumb fuck, you killed my dog!!!"

I really thought I had something to do with it, so I kept trying to say I was sorry, but all that would come out was inaudible sobbing. He picked up the small dog by its back legs; it lay lifeless in the air. The next thing I saw was the drooping jaw of the dog fly to my face with such force that it knocked my tiny, naked body back to the floor. I lay there and tried to curl up to block the blows of the man hitting me with the dead animal, cussing all the while. The tooth from the dog's upper jaw was sticking out a small bit, so the last blow he struck caused my face to trickle warm blood. He finally subsided, yelled for me to put my clothes on and go straight to the living room and sleep on the pee-stained couch by the old TV.

I got up, and much like the dog who was full of life an hour ago, I limped all the way into the cold house. The last I remember was crying on the couch and waking up the next day to Mom being mad at me. The story (as he told it) was that I had been picking at the dog on purpose to make it angry, and the dog retaliated by biting my face. The only way to get it off of me was to kill what happened to be one of his favorite dogs. I wanted to say my plea and give the real account, but as soon as he saw my intention, he shot me a glance so cold it could have made a desert freeze.

I was at a loss. He was the hero for saving me; I was the bratty kid for picking on the dog; Mom was mad at me for trying to ruin every relationship she ever had.

These types of situations continued for months and months, but one day Mom finally awoke from her drunken slumber. I'm not sure if she saw me, but what she did see made her leave that cold autumn night. It was her pet cat being held against a fence while he took a hammer and repeatedly slammed the life from her. As soon as Mom started yelling, I ran back to the living room. She almost immediately came to scoop me up, and we got into the car and drove back to the trailer on the hill.

That was the last night I ever had to see him, and I was thankful for that. It was definitely too much to comprehend then, and is almost too much to comprehend now. I can't change it, but I can grow away from the hatred and anger that this memory has built up inside of me.

With God's grace.

*Dear Father,

I've looked for you for a long time. As a kid, I thought that each new man that came into the yellow-stained walls of my trailer house, might be the person that I clung to. I thought the next one might be one that taught me how to throw a curve ball in the front yard, change oil or fix a flat tire and all those basic necessities of growing up and becoming a man.

Each time you failed me. You made me feel worthless. You abused me. You tore my heart up with words and actions so unthinkable I blocked them, clear into my adult years. I needed you and you were not there. I lost hope in finding you. I remember the day I found out my wife was pregnant, wishing you had been there to prepare me for that moment. When I would become the thing I so longed to have. I had no clue what to do, how to be, or even my purpose in this child's life. I despised you, and most of the time I hated you. I was pissed that you never taught me how to love and care for another human—How to lift up and raise a child with morals and instill worth. I was so bitter I couldn't see the truth.

When I finally stopped looking for you, I realized the father I was searching for existed. He has been living inside of me. Every demeaning word that was planted in my heart, from your mouth, was a lesson in what words NOT to use to my son. Every birthday you didn't show up to, was a reminder of how much the memories we make in these moments matter. Every ounce of love that I didn't receive from you, helps me to see and acknowledge the love I have for my own child every day.

*So to you, my nonexistent biological father, I say, you are forgiven. Thank you for letting me see the qualities that I will try every day to deter from. I thank you for the search in finding a worldly father, because in doing so, I have found something richer. I have found **God the Father**, a dad that has never failed me—A father that loves unconditionally, and inspires me to do the same. The huge failure from my worldly dad, teaches me that my minor failures as a father are ok. I turned out ok and by grace, so will my son. I'm thankful to be surrounded by friends who are fathers who show this same kind of love to their children. To be inspired by and learn from each other has been a solid foundation to becoming the father I have so desperately searched for all these years.*

Lastly, I want to say you were wrong. I am worthy. I am a good father. And I am capable of raising-up and influencing the next generation that will be free from your lies. I will make mistakes, but unlike you, I will own up to them, ask for forgiveness, and learn every day to be a better father than the day before.

Your worldy-worthy son,

Tim

Jerry

Great—a new man.

What horrible thing will I have to endure with him around?

Not only was he new, but he was a square. And he was old...like, really old. He was a DJ at a local radio station and had a gospel music hour. Southern gospel at that, which sounded like a bunch of old hillbillies trying to bang out praises to God on the back porch of a ranch house—not something any kid would ever be interested in having to listen to. The main turn-off about him was that he tried to enforce rules and regulations into our daily lives, which had been typically fine with us doing what we pleased, when we pleased. I knew it would be a phase though, just like all the other terrible men who came around.

Again, I was proven wrong. He was here for the long haul and no matter how much I hated that, I was going to have to deal.

A few months later, we had to dress like we were respectable little kids and put on some of the most hideous, hand-me-down suits from Goodwill. The smell protruding from them would have been enough to kill a small family of skunks. We walked to the front row of a rundown church built in a secluded wooded area too many years ago to count, and watched the marriage take place. My brothers already knew the drill, but it was a first for me, so I was constantly getting scolded by Granny.

"Be quiet and stop wiggling!"

It was the beginning of something that would grow into reasons why we stayed alive. Even though no one liked this new man, good things happened as a result of him being with us. Mom no longer had her weird friends over to do even weirder things in our living room.

I guessed that was a plus...for now.

Step-dad 1980 - Something

CHAPTER TWO
The Farmhouse

Bookstore Night

Since Mom had been in a Satanic cult for most of my life, we didn't play around with supernatural things. Whether it was a Ouija board, or even scary movies, we weren't allowed to watch or play in any sort of way with those types of things. EVER. When we asked why, the only answer we got was that it opened doors to allow things into your mind that ought not be there. This was such a big deal to Mom that it sometimes seemed the things we had to do were very irrational, even to my underdeveloped mind.

One night as we were getting ready for bed, I could hear Mom screaming through the thin walls. A few minutes later, Stepdad told us to grab our sleeping bags and all the cushions off the couch and load them into the truck. Mom was crying and kept saying, "They're coming! They're almost here!"

We drove so quickly into town that it seemed like we flew there, my brothers bouncing from side to side in the pillow-cushioned truck bed at every turn. We stopped at the bookstore covered in religious paraphernalia--Bibles, cassette tapes, t-shirts and even stuffed Noah's Ark toys from front to back. We lay down on pallets scattered in sporadic order on the floor and tried to fall asleep, but were stopped by Mom screaming and crying, saying she could see them. What "them" were, I had no clue, but the fear in her voice caused my own imagination to make me just as (or even more) scared than she. As I looked toward the high windows of the storefront, I thought I saw what she was scared of...and she had good reason.

There was a cloud of blackness swirling and hovering about every window, swooping and clouding our view of the moonlight. It didn't have the shape of any human or animal--it was its own smoky, iridescent being. I had seen these same types of images before, but not to this extent. It was as if there were a hundred of them morphed together to form an ultimately evil and dark being, capable of causing fear in the hardest mind. My mouth dropped and I froze in fear, wanting to scream and run. Having no control over my body, I did nothing.

When I looked back at Mom, the black shapes seemed to be swirling above her body too. After a few minutes she began to speak in an almost dreamlike sleep state. At first it was really low, like the growl of a dog with indistinguishable words. Then, as she got louder and louder, she began screaming, and her whole body was thrown to the floor. Stepdad was now in front of her with our pastor (whom I didn't even see come in), and Pastor was talking to her in a stern voice.

"I cast you out in the name of Jesus!!" were the words I could make out, and after that, he would speak so fast that I couldn't understand if it was even in English. Each time he would start these phrases, Mom would scream louder, "NO!!!" and her body would twist and contort as if she was being tortured. Something that she couldn't control was making her body shake.

After a few minutes of watching this take place, you could feel the air, the tinge of the room, get so cold that every hair on my body that could be seen was standing straight up. The yelling bout finally ended when Pastor yelled one final "BE GONE!!!" At the same moment, a shriek-like scream of anger that was not human nor animal ricocheted off every wall and window in the bookstore. Mom fell to the ground face first with a deep, defeated sob.

When I finally obtained control over my body, I did the only thing I knew how to do to deal with fear—hide. I ducked my face into the covers and squeezed my eyes shut to the point that I thought they might burst out of my ears. Within a few minutes I had fallen into a much-needed dream that didn't have anything remotely scary or evil in it.

The next day when we awoke, Mom had our clothes sitting out at our feet where we lay. We got dressed without mentioning anything that had happened the night before or what we had seen. We were taken to school as awkwardly and quickly as possible, with no explanations. My mind was racing, but since no one else said anything, I took the hint and said nothing myself. The whole day went by at school with me not focusing on anything but those images I had seen the night before.

What the heck was going on?

Grandpa's Smile

The man I admired most.

The man with all the answers to every question I had ever asked.

The strongest person on the face of the earth.

Although he seemed mostly happy all my life, this was the day I saw him truly smile. We had been visiting him all week in the hospital, but he must have just been really tired every time we were there. His mind would periodically float in and out of consciousness, and I would receive a "hi" or "hey boy".

These visits were useless and of no point to me. What fun was there in not playing games and going on adventures with the person who I knew was the best at it? This didn't seem to matter to Mom though. I guess fun is different as you get older.

This went on for weeks, and I finally got so tired of it that I started trying different ways of amusing myself. There were a ton of gadgets and weirdly shaped objects to play with, pretending I was a doctor as well. Finally, after a few times of clumsily knocking things off shelves and out of drawers, I had gotten my wish of not having to go up there anymore. This was great news for me because it gave me more time to explore the field by my house alone while everyone else was stuck at the nauseatingly boring hospital.

I awoke on a Wednesday morning to Mom crying over my shoulder, telling me I needed to go tell Grandpa goodbye. I was crushed, immediately thinking of how much I had been looking forward to walking down to the murky pond on the other side of the barn today. I grudgingly did as I was told, got into the car and started pouting.

I noticed this trip was a little different though. Instead of passing by this certain field of cows and horses, we bypassed it to go in a totally different direction. I knew then where we were going—this was the way to Granny's house. I knew it because we would pass the same 100-year old oak tree with branches stretching out so far as if to hug the sun. I didn't want to jinx myself, but my insides knew this had all been a trick to surprise me!

Sure enough, a few minutes later we pulled up the steep driveway leading to their house. As we walked in, I was told to be very quiet. I saw all of my uncles and my one aunt in the living room, surrounding the same type of bed that Grandpa had been lying on for weeks. I thought this was a little strange and had to take a closer peek.

Grandpa was there, yet it wasn't the same Grandpa I remembered seeing. His face was sunken in, and his eyes closed so loosely that you couldn't tell if he was pretend sleeping or just in such a deep sleep that he couldn't help it. Everyone around him had tear-filled eyes, loaded and ready to pour out. Uncle began talking to someone who wasn't even in the room named "Heavenly Father". Everyone in the room closed their eyes and looked down toward their feet, loosing the dam that had been holding back their tears. I was the only one in the room with eyes open, peering at everyone with curiosity. What was happening?

I started to ask Grandpa what was going on, but was silenced at once by Mom's hand over my face and a stern "Shhhh!" As soon as Uncle stopped talking, everyone opened their now puffy red eyes and looked at Grandpa. I saw Grandpa struggle to open both eyes as wide as he could, as if there were tiny weights sitting on each lid. He lifted one hand up a few inches, then I saw it—the biggest smile that had ever graced his face. He was so noticeably happy that I began laughing for no good reason at all. As quickly as the smile had come, it was gone again. His eyes closed and his arm lay flat by his side once more.

The tears came stronger with Mom, Granny, and Aunt. Even some of my uncles seemed to be letting their tears flow freely. I now knew something big was happening, and I guess the emotions spread around the room were contagious because I started crying too. This was the last time I would see Grandpa, and something inside me knew this even though my brain couldn't comprehend it.

APR 1968

my grandpa

my hero

80's galveston vacation

Knife Fight

By now I was used to seeing things that were out of the norm. From something really awkward and hateful being said, to a situation where you didn't know if the people you were watching would still be alive after it was over, out of the norm was the norm to me.

This was one of those nights.

The Rule Man, Stepdad, was trying to up his game by actually enforcing rules on us. This might have flown if we were all still babies, but we were getting to the point where we were angry kids, and for my brothers, angry pre-teens. We had concrete attitudes and ways we thought that were set in stone, and now there wasn't ANYONE who could try and make us do something we didn't want to do.

It was close to 11 pm on a school night, and my brothers wanted to ride into town on their beat-up bikes to go to the local 24-hour gas station. Since we lived so far out of town, the gas station with its many assortments of candies, gums, and sodas was more like an amusement park for kids with pockets full of change.

Stepdad had different plans. He told all of us to get straight to bed so we would be able to get up without any problems in the morning. I had had a hard day of playing video games and watching cartoons, so I didn't have any contest with the request. In a light, non-aggressive manner, my brothers just started saying that they would go to bed as soon as they got back from the store. This quickly escalated when they were cut off in mid-sentence with a firm "NO"; that is when things started to get out of hand.

Yelling was coming from both sides, and then my brothers started cussing. Whack!! A hand went right across my brother's butt. This being Oldest Brother and happening in front of everyone, it immediately caused embarrassment, then intense anger. He was nearly a teenager and had gotten a spanking from the person he despised more than anyone else. Oldest Brother shoved Stepdad so hard that he fell onto the pool table. The colored balls left on the table flew from side to side, bouncing off the embankments. Stepdad grabbed Oldest by his collar, shoved him into his old room downstairs by the staircase and slammed the door shut behind him. The door opened to the outside, so every few seconds you could see the oldest, slamming his body into the door as it opened a few inches, pushing against Stepdad's weight. After what seemed like a few minutes, there was silence on both sides of the now slightly cracked door.

Then, when Stepdad had relaxed his weight on holding the door, there was one final blow. The door was knocked to the side with a loud sound of cracking wood, and Oldest flew out like a bull out of its stable. He had knocked Stepdad to the floor and was now on top of him, using every inch of his strength to keep the man pinned down. There was something in his hand. It was a shining silver blade attached to a gold-colored metal handle with holes running vertically down each side—the butterfly knife he had bought at an Army Navy Store downtown. The blade was inches from Stepdad's face, shaking with all the force of strength that Oldest could summon. Stepdad might have been bigger and stronger, but in his position now, Oldest actually had the upper hand, even with his disadvantages.

This was one of the times I just froze and didn't have the will or strength to say even one word. I just stood there, still as a broken action figure, watching in awe. Older Brother was screaming at both of them, telling Oldest it wasn't worth it. Mom then came into the picture, and pushed and pulled on Oldest until the knife came down so forcefully it stabbed a few inches into the wood underneath the stained carpet. Stepdad was free and so was my brother.

Mom yelled at everyone watching to go to bed "NOW!!" In the heat of the ending of it all, defeated Oldest stormed out the side door as quickly as he could, knife in hand and tears of anger flowing. By the time Stepdad could get to him, he was already halfway down the driveway on his tiny, worn bike. As Stepdad stood in the yard watching him fly off, I felt that a pursuit would proceed to take place, but instead he came back inside a few minutes later with four beat-up, slightly warped nails and our old hammer. Since the locks on our door had been broken, Stepdad took matters into his own hands and placed a nail diagonal to the top corner of the door and began hammering.

"No one goes in or out tonight!" And no one even tried after that.

I'm not sure where my biggest brother went on that bike of his, but we didn't see him for at least three days. When he finally did show his face, it was as if nothing had happened. He came in the side door, went straight to our under-crowded fridge, poured a glass of milk (probably expired), and went to his room upstairs. Nothing was said by him and nothing was said by Stepdad.

I guess if you wait long enough, problems will just fade away.

The Cookie Truck Incident

One thing I noticed about Stepdad is that he always had a new job. Radio DJ, Christian bookstore, selling meat, selling shoes, selling insurance...and these were just in the first year that we knew him.

I think our favorite job that he ever had was at a cookie company. He would go around to different grocery stores in the area and be their supplier for a certain brand of cookies. The reason we liked it so much was because he would get to take the company truck home every night. It was a big, box-shaped truck with a smiley-faced lady on the side of it. In the back was an assortment of cookies fit for a king! Chocolate chip, sugar, snickerdoodle, vanilla wafers...you name it; it was back there.

One summer Stepdad brought home a free-standing swimming pool that he had gotten from a vendor friend. Circular in shape and about twelve feet across, it had a big picture of a red Coke bottle on it. As it came in a few pieces, we were all getting it out of the back of the truck. One box held the pump, another the plastic ladder to get in and out, and another had the actual pool in it. After we had taken the pool to the backyard to get it ready for swimming, the oldest ones decided to play a joke on Brother. I was just glad they were doing it to him and not to me this time, so I went with them as they prepared.

They asked him to get a certain box of cookies (that really didn't even exist) out of the front part of the truck. After he got all the way in, submerged in cookies and trying to find an imaginary box, they shut the back door. They then turned the metal handle at the bottom of the door to lock him inside. All we could hear after that was his yelling and beating on the back door of the truck, begging us to let him out. We all laughed and mocked him for a few minutes until I started feeling sympathetic. He sounded really upset and almost in tears. I started to unlatch the lock and was stopped in my tracks by a slap to the back of my head. I knew my brothers weren't done toying with him yet, and there was nothing in my power to change their minds; I was then under their orders not to touch the lock.

A few minutes later, we all heard Stepdad yelling for us to bring him the water hose so we could start filling up the pool. Of course, our attention spans being the length of a small thread, we all began running at once, excited by the thought of getting to swim. We had been filling up the pool for almost an hour when we were asked where Brother was.

Everyone's faces sunk low, knowing that they had forgotten about him in the back of the truck. We were about to be in big trouble. This face was noticeable, even to our very unobservant stepdad, and he pressed harder for more information. I was the first to crack.

"Maybe...he might be in the cookie truck?"

As he walked us all to the front of the house, he saw the truck with the lock latched but stopped and listened. Brother's weak whimpers were coming through the cracks of the truck.

Stepdad immediately opened it up and found Brother, completely soaked in sweat and tears, bright as the reddest marker I had ever seen. It was at least 100 degrees outside, but inside the steaming metal truck, the temperatures must have been at least 50 degrees higher. My stomach immediately sank, and I felt sick for not helping him out of there sooner. I think my brothers felt the same way because they were apologizing over and over, and it actually sounded sincere.

Stepdad just looked at us and shook his head. He didn't have to say anything.

After a few hours of lying down in front of an old, dusty box fan, his color regained its natural tint. He was the only one who got to swim in the pool for the first week we had it, and even though I would have given anything to swim right then, I knew we deserved the punishment.

sorry, brother :)

Stolen Wagon

There were nights when Stepdad would be gone, Mom would pass out early and us kids would have the run of the house. Actually this was quite a few nights, but on this particular night, my brothers thought it would be a good idea to play racecars.

Now this wasn't your ordinary, Nascar-style racing machine that they would be using. It was a light blue, seven-passenger, 1980-something Ford station wagon, capable of speeds close to or exceeding fifty-five miles an hour. It was a mean chunk of metal...so we thought. We all piled into the stench-stained car, Oldest Brother behind the wheel, Neighbor in the cockpit, and the rest of us in the back. I was in the seat farthest in the back, which faced the rear window. This was my favorite place to sit because of the view.

We started at a speed fitting for an airplane takeoff. I had to stop my head from hitting the back window every time the car would make its robotic, jumpy stops, mostly because Oldest would have to stretch a little to reach the full extent of the brakes, then scoot back up to see over the dashboard. We made a few laps around the neighborhood with my brothers hanging their heads out of the windows, screaming profanities to no one and laughing all the while. I have to admit, it was actually really relaxing for me. I just sat back there, staring at the stars, connecting them like a dot-to-dot drawing, making castles and animal shapes of all kinds.

Toward the end of this trip, my brothers decided to test the limit on how fast they could go in reverse. They would pull all the way to the end of the street adjacent to our driveway, slam it in reverse, and whoever had the top speed by the time they hit the driveway was the winner. Oldest went first and managed to beat his top score of thirty-four miles an hour, so this set the next driver up for quite a challenge. As we started barreling down the short strip of street, I felt the wheels get unsteady and just knew we were about to fly off the road. Oldest Brother quickly over-corrected the problem, slammed on the brakes, and we were spinning.

SLAM!! The sound of an elephant running straight into a tin bar is what I heard. When I opened my eyes, we were somehow completely lined up with the driveway as Oldest slowly crept the car into it. We all jumped out to see what had happened; a mailbox with the numbers 1-2-3 on it was laying in the over-grown grass in front of our house. Everyone instantly burst out in laughter. For some reason, we all thought this was the funniest thing we had seen and done all year long.

The tank of a car had a tiny scratch on the back end,

not the same car, but man did we love driving

only noticeable to someone if you pointed it out with a microscope. The mailbox, on the other hand, was a completely opposite story. The wood pole that once held it upright was completely broken in half, and the metal portion where the mail goes was dented as if someone had...well, slammed into it with a car! There weren't many things that could wake Mom from a sleep like she was in, but that sound obviously did. She came out screaming.

"What is going on?!"

My brothers, being the fast thinkers they were, said that someone just drove by, swerving all over the road, and knocked the mailbox down. To add to the lie, there were very distant taillights on the main highway. We all started pointing at them and explaining all at once. So instead of being in trouble, we were consoled and asked if we were ok.

It was a nice end to a very funny night.

UFO

On most nights when Mom said she saw something fly by her window or a little man run by the door, we would just simply let it go in one ear and out the other. She must have had sharper vision than anyone else in the house, because she saw a lot of things that we couldn't see with our weak and feeble eyes.

One time was different though. I saw the something too.

We were outside on the porch around 8 pm, spitting sunflower seeds into the over-grown grass. Cousin was in the bath filled with bubbles and G.I. Joes. Brothers were having a Super Mario marathon in the next room. Out of nowhere, we saw a light in the sky that at first just looked like a star. It began to grow; apparently this was no star. We saw it zoom from one side of the sky to the other in a split second, leaving a trace of bright light as it went.

As fast as she could, Mom called all the boys outside—even Cousin came, wrapped in a red, ratty towel, hair full of bubbles. We piled into the blue station wagon and Mom drove in the direction of the light, staring up out of the window, swerving all over the blacktop road.

We came to an open field where we could see it—a shadowed, circular object, no more than a hundred feet above the ground. There was a fog of painted colors coming out from below where its shadow ended. We all stared in amazement, wondering who or what this thing was. As quickly as it had shown itself, it vanished, leaving only a trace of smoke. We drove around for at least an hour trying to find it again, but we never did.

Could it have been our imaginations? Yes, quite possibly, but I've seen a lot weirder stuff than this, so I'll choose to believe it was something bigger than just imagination.

Why not?

The Window

It was a Friday night and the wind outside was seeping into the crevices of every window. We had rented the Nintendo game Paperboy and been playing it for the last few hours while snacking on cardboard HyTop pizzas and Doritos—a typical weekend night. Except there was a definite eeriness in the air. We had felt it all night; but brothers and me hadn't voiced it.

I heard a sudden slam against the front porch, so I carefully went to the door and peeped my head out, only to see a wooden flower box dumped over. I thought it was most likely from the strong winds, trying to shake the feeling and get back to my game. There was still something not right...and then, out of the corner of my eye, I saw it. I was almost scared to turn and confirm what my vision was seeing, thinking that if I blocked it out, it would go away. I guess the same image had crept into Brother's vision too, because we both looked around at the same time to the exact same spot in the window.

A face with dark eyes was peering through the foggy, dirt-covered pane. This wasn't just any face; it was the kind that made you feel hate and fear so intensely that you just knew you were in danger.

Brother grabbed the first thing he saw, which happened to be a dark green, number six pool ball from the table beside the TV. It shattered the window, but we didn't see if it made contact with the man outside. At the sound of broken glass, Stepdad and Mom came bursting through the door, wondering what we had broken. We told them what had happened, and were told to go to the one bedroom upstairs and lock the door. Thirty minutes later, we saw the lights of police cars pull up to the house and heard the men talking indistinctly downstairs. I could hear Mom's voice sounding as if she were trying not to cry, but I could not understand the words she was saying. Stepdad came up a little later and told us we didn't have to be worried anymore, that the cop would stay parked in the neighborhood until morning to make sure no one came back.

I know it was years later, but the face I saw had the same hollow eyes that I remembered seeing in the graveyard so much earlier. I'm not sure if it was the same person, but it was definitely the same type of person. When I looked into his eyes, I didn't see anyone inside looking back.

Just a hollow, dark hole.

Flipped Out

When we said the words "Mom's flipped out," all in the house knew what that meant.

No doctors had a truly accurate answer of why it happened, except that there was a tiny spot on Mom's brain that was a little off balance. What it meant to us was that we had to fend for ourselves when she was flipped out--whether it was making something to eat, getting to the store or even just basic knowledge questions. The spot on her brain would be off balance if she didn't take her medicine, or sometimes when she would, but mix it with liquor or some pain-relieving drug. Her brain would revert back to that of a seventeen year old, and she would think it was 1967.

We used to think it was fake until it happened while she was driving home one night. Her brain shut off and she flipped out while going down the highway. We flew off the road into a ditch; she hadn't learned to drive a car until she was twenty-seven, ten years after where she was in her mind. Older Brother had experienced this more than anyone, usually on his way home from karate classes he took in town, so he knew what to do. He would push her aside to the passenger seat and drive us home. Actually, he was a smoother driver than Mom was when she was in her right mind, so the transition wasn't bad at all! We learned not to let her drive at night as much as possible to avoid these kinds of accidents.

A funny thing we would do is tell her that we were from the future, showing her pennies with 1992 written on them and dollars from 1988. She would always be really impressed and ask us funny questions. We would fill her with some of the wildest stories of spacemen and flying cars! We figured we might as well have some fun with it.

Arrox. age mom thought she was

The main downfall was that she was still into the Satanic culture when she was seventeen. Mixed with the schizophrenia, that could sometimes make for very unstable moments, with voices telling her to do things that hurt us. We tried to avoid that at all cost, even if it meant leaving and riding our bikes for hours until she fell asleep.

We were definitely kept on our toes during those nights.

Ants on Fire

If there's one thing that has always intrigued me, it would be fire—the sound of it, the smell of it as you burn things, even the warmth you get from being near it. Combining my love of fire with my hatred of ants became a favorite pastime for me and my brothers.

This one steamy, muggy summer, we came across a bed of ants the size of a small sand castle. We knew we would need more than the typical lighter and newspaper for this job. Brother headed for the peeled-paint garage to grab the red metal can of gas as I headed to the bathroom for the oversized AquaNet can. By the time I got there, Brother had almost completely soaked the hill with gasoline and was ready for ignition. We had a box of strike anywhere matches to start the blaze.

As soon as we dropped the first match, a heated explosion of fire flew up and burned the tiny hairs on our arms, retracting each one into singed follicles. The heat from the sun mixed with the heat of the flames, causing us to sweat and feel sticky. I saw a fleet of ants trying to escape, so I grabbed my trusty hairspray can and started going to town. The reaction from the flammable spray coming out and the engulfing fire was a spectacle in itself.

This went on until the can was completely empty, and I got the smart idea of putting it on top of a hill to make a bomb. We ran out of harm's way and waited for the blast. Before we got more than a few feet away, the can soared like a burning missile into the air, landing in the field to the left of the anthill. As soon as it came in contact with the overly dry grass, there was an immediate reaction—the flames spread and spread fast! We saw what was happening and went to get buckets of water from inside the house to put it out. By the time we got back, our buckets were not enough to even put a dent in this flame. We came up with a plan as quickly as we could, taking our cutoff blue jean shorts and soaking them in the water from our buckets. Then we grabbed our shorts at the legs and started beating the fire with the butt pocket portion of the soaked jeans. It seemed to be working!

We were working as fast as we could and were starting to see results, when out of nowhere; a huge wind gust burst though the flames. Our efforts were in vain as the wind took what little fire was left and multiplied it times ten. Our only option now was to grab the burned up hairspray can, throw it underneath the porch, put the gas can back into the garage...and then run in and pretend we knew nothing about it.

A neighbor was driving by and called the fire department. Ten minutes later a crew was there, extinguishing the flames. By the time they finished, there was nothing left but a black square the size of a football field. Since all evidence of our having anything to do with the accident was hidden out of sight, it was blamed on a cigarette being thrown out into the field.

Which was fine by me.

Wrecked

Stepdad had driven three hours in our red Chevy pickup to buy all the fryers, metal tanks and stoves needed to start a small Mexican restaurant. We were in school while he did this, then got dropped off at the bookstore where Mom was working. When the day was coming to a close, he pulled up with a trailer full of stuff. I had no idea what it did, but it was still exciting nonetheless.

Two Oldest Brothers had ridden their bikes home from school, so it was just me and Closest Brother who would be riding home with Mom and Stepdad. We begged to ride home inside one of the metal tanks on the wooden trailer attached to the truck. It looked like a spaceship, making it all the more appealing. Ten minutes of hassling and the best we could get was to ride in the bed of the truck. We weren't completely happy with this compromise, but it was better than being squished in the front seat. On the way home we would pretend that we were Army men inside a GI vehicle, shooting snipers in the woods as we passed. The ride was five miles from the store to our home base, so we got a lot of shooting practice on the way. For the last two or three miles, there was a small, faded black truck following us very closely---we just knew it was the Cobra Kahn.

As we made it to our street, we saw the truck speed up even faster. I was on the right side, so I saw what was about to happen, but instead of yelling to Brother, I froze.

Then the impact.

The tiny black vehicle struck the side of the truck where Brother was sitting, knocking him forward into one of the metal tables. I then saw everything in slow motion.

We were spinning horizontally as the black truck ricocheted into the trailer, causing it and all the equipment to swing unhitched into the ditch. I looked up to see the entire truck fly over my head, exposing metal pipes and tubes usually unseen by anyone but mechanics. Then one final thud as the hood of the black truck lay upside down on our hood. There was a cloud of smoke as things started to resume their regular speed.

Through the smoke, I saw the body of a man on the ground beside the truck; blood was covering all the parts of his body that I could see. I didn't know what to do, so I just ran to the only place I thought was safe—the house. Since we were already on our street, it was clearly the only logical thing I could make my body do. Which also turned out to be a bad idea, because I was in trouble when I was finally found, curled up on my porch, crying. They had been looking on both sides of the ditch for my body to be like the one I saw before I bolted.

I was checked for breaks and cuts, but they found only a few small scratches. We had gotten lucky, but that wasn't the case for the two in the black truck. I found out later that the one I saw didn't make it, and the one driving was paralyzed from the impact. Stepdad didn't have any insurance on all that equipment he had bought; the only things salvageable were some metal tables.

The restaurant was just another failed attempt to make ends meet.

Geronimo

Our big house was getting even bigger. The attic, which was tall enough for grown men to play basketball in, was finally going to be used to its full potential. In order to do this, we had to find someone who actually had the knowledge and the muscle to take on such a task.

His name was Geronimo, and for a good while he lived in our attic.

Apparently, he had been there for a while without me even knowing. When I first saw him, he was in the yard, stealing our flowers. I began throwing rocks at him and yelling, "Get out of here!"

Mom came out and started scolding. I tried to tell her about how he was stealing, but was cut off by her explanation.

"He works for us and is helping build a room for you upstairs. And he is NOT stealing flowers; he's plucking the weeds that are around the flowers. Grow a brain, Child!"

I instantly felt two inches tall, thinking I was doing good and getting shut down again. Geronimo then stuck his hand out as I flinched for fear of his retaliation on my rock throwing. Instead he motioned for my hand.

"I, Geronimo; you must be Timoteo."

I started to laugh at the way that sounded, but stopped abruptly, realizing that he wasn't mad at me for throwing things at him. Someone forgiving you without an apology was noticeably nice, even at my young age. From then on out, I tried to help with anything he was doing, most of the time probably just getting in the way, but he never told me if I was. He was always just grateful for my efforts. At times he would show me different tricks and ways to fold money to make it look like airplanes or t-shirts. He even had money that was not in the same language as the money we used! A lot of good times were had in that house while he lived and worked there.

The first upstairs room was built that would belong to Two Oldest Brothers, and then things were put on hold. Geronimo went to Mexico to visit family for Christmas, and we never saw him again. Stepdad later found out that he didn't have some colored card that lets you come and go as you please to anywhere in the world. For the next few months, I looked around the house for a green, square card that he might've lost while he was there, but it was to no avail.

It looked like I had lost a friend...as well as the chance of ever having my own bedroom.

Nestle Coco

Sometimes I find myself angry and torn up inside, looking back at the way things could've been. But then there are the situations where I see how funny my life could have been too.

On my seventh birthday, I was awakened in the morning by the image of a balding man nudging me to get up, silvery gray patches on each side of his head. Stepdad told me he had a present for me in the barn, to get up and come see it. I got up, put on my worn out, black Converse and trudged through the dewy field, getting the bottom hem of my pajama pants soaking wet. When we got inside the hay-filled barn, Stepdad stopped me and said, "Ok, what you're about to get is a gift, but it's also a test of responsibility and the ability to be a good worker. Do you think you are up to the task? Because if you're not, I need to know now. "

My curiosity was at peak level now; there was no way I was going to say no to an offer like that! As I agreed blindly to do a task that I would never find out how hard it actually was. I was led around to a corral that looked almost empty. Then I saw it--a chocolate brown calf right in the corner. Its legs were thin and boney, much like my own. As I saw it, my excitement level went through the roof. I screamed, "Whoa!! What the heck is that, a mini cow?"

He then explained that it was a baby calf, and its mother had died giving birth to it. I would have to be this calf's mom now. I would have to come out here at the dawn of each day to feed it with a bottle, nursing it to health at least four times a day. I didn't realize how much work that actually entailed at the time, and I didn't care. I was stoked! I got to give it a name of my choice—Nestle Coco, but I just called her Coco for short.

Over the next few days I formed a bond with her and was excited to go out every day to feed and take care of her. Around the fourth day, I went to try and feed her the bottle before the sun came out, but she wouldn't take it. I just figured it was because it was so early; she was getting stronger and didn't feel the need to eat that early anymore. I waited until the midday feeding, but she still wasn't hungry. I started getting worried that I wasn't doing my job right, but didn't want to tell anyone in case I would be relieved of my duties. I loved this cow and wasn't going to let anyone take it from me because I couldn't take care of it properly.

The entire day went by and not one feeding would she take. I figured I would just try again the next day and fell asleep. I must have overslept, because I awoke to that same image of the balding man in my sleep-worn face. This time he didn't seem as happy, so I immediately awoke and started clumsily putting my shoes on to go out to the barn. Before I could even get the first shoe on, he said he had some bad news for me. He told me that Coco was not going to live much longer. She had contracted some kind of disease and was in an extreme amount of pain. He then told me I would have to take responsibility for helping her to stop hurting. I guessed I was going to have to feed her some kind of medicine.

We both walked to the barn, much slower and more somber feeling this time. When we got there, Coco could barely walk and her mouth was opening and closing as if she were trying to speak to us. The sound wasn't words, but you could tell it was a sad story. We walked her to the back of the barn where there was light breaking through the sky from the beginning of the sunlight. Stepdad handed me the same tool that I had seen in my First Memory, told me to aim it right at the calf's head and pull the lever on the bottom.

I didn't know exactly what would happen, but my gut feeling knew it would be bad. I started crying and say, "No, I don't want to!"

Then he reminded me of the promise I had made him on the day that I met Coco. My pleas were of no use, and eventually I took the rifle from him. It was heavy and cold and almost too much for my fragile body to handle as I weaved and bobbed around, catching my balance. He positioned the rifle, holding the barrel with my puny, shaky left hand and letting it rest on my right shoulder. I counted to three as directed and pulled the trigger. The same familiar booming sound was back, but this time I was knocked on the ground. The butt end of the gun had bounced so hard into my shoulder that it immediately started bruising as I lay in a pile of dry hay. When I finally got back to my feet, tears flowing down, I saw her lying there. She only moved for a few seconds, and then was completely still. I had killed the only thing I had ever been in control of. I got reassuring "good jobs" from Stepdad, but it didn't make what I did feel any better.

This would haunt me for a lot of my life, but I couldn't tell anyone I was upset about it for fear of being made fun of by my brothers. Needless to say, I never wanted to take care of any animal from then on.

And to think I could have been the type of guy who rides bulls for fun or goes to shows to present my prize heifer! That's the part that makes me laugh.

CHAPTER THREE
House on the Highway

Moving time again.

This time I wasn't as happy about it because it felt like we were downgrading. The house was only one story and about half the size of our big house on the farm. It was barren, windows almost non-existent.

The one plus was that this house came with my very own trampoline in the backyard. A lot of my life was spent on that thing—jumping, sleeping, playing Gameboy. One instance in particular would turn out to be one of the most life-changing experiences I've ever had...

Trampoline

Now that Mom had a higher paying job and knew someone who sold satellites, we were able to freely watch cartoons at any time of the day. Stepdad worked for a steel-toe boot company, selling shoes in parking lots all over Dallas. He had been out of town for about five days when I feel asleep during a marathon of Tom & Jerry. When I awoke to the sound of a frying pan being hit on the TV, there was no one around.

I searched every room for signs of life, but all were vacant. I walked around outside and finally heard laughter and talk coming from the backyard. My brothers were on the trampoline with Mom, giggling and blowing smoke out of their mouths from a tiny white and yellow-tinted cigarette.

I had seen Mom smoke these a ton of times in the past, but this was the first time I saw her share with my brothers. Curiosity and a need to be part of this family gathering took hold of my body as I ran and jumped on the side of the trampoline closest to Mom. They all immediately yelled at me, asking what I thought I was doing. I started to whine and tell them it wasn't fair, when Mom stopped everyone by yelling, "Calm down! Let him in the circle."

She said she wasn't going to have us kill her buzz—whatever that meant.

She knew I wouldn't relent until I had tried the same thing Bigger Brothers were doing...and she was right. She passed me the cigarette; I felt its bumpy, ridged surface through my fingers. I was told to suck on it like a straw, then blow the smoke out slowly. As I started to inhale as deeply as possible, the smoke felt like needles piercing the back of my tiny throat. As soon as the smoke went in, it came out, with me coughing and gagging on every wisp. Brothers laughed, as well as Mom, but I didn't see what was funny. After my coughing fit was over, I was told to try it again, but not suck in so hard this time. I tried three or four more puffs, but every time it was the same result. I said I didn't want to try anymore and handed it back to Mom. I didn't feel as bad when I saw her start coughing in the same manner that I had minutes earlier.

Smoke filled the scenery surrounding us, and it wasn't long before I started feeling more relaxed than I had ever felt in my entire life. Everything seemed to flow as slow as honey, with thoughts seeping through each pore of my mind; soon I was laughing uncontrollably too. I felt hunger come over me like a beast in the jungle that hadn't eaten in days, so I scooted off the trampoline and went back into the house to devour some prey. With a mouthful of cookies, I lay back on the floor in front of the TV and slowly floated into one of the most vivid, imaginative dreams I had ever had.

This would be the start of my nights, my family meetings, on that trampoline.

Tennis Balls

So...how do I say this without sounding like an episode of The Beverly Hillbillies? Brother's dad is his second cousin, first removed, twice backwards. No, or was it his first cousin, second uncle?

This makes it easier—his dad was Mom's cousin. Or if that is too much to comprehend, it means some of the branches in this family tree are definitely swinging in the wrong direction.

Needless to say, there were some birth defects that caused him problems early on in life. He had to get a metal plate inserted in his forehead because he was born without a soft spot. This might have made it difficult for him, but for us, it added to some of the fun we had as kids. At least once a week, we would wake up before he did and grab the flat, fruit-shaped magnets off the dirty yellow fridge. Then we would place them sporadically on his forehead without waking him.

He was a very unobservant person, and by "very", I mean that I don't think he even knew what a mirror was. He just sprayed some spritz on his hair, put his clothes on and walked out the door. Walking out to the bus stop, we all would be laughing at what he thought were faces we made, but in reality it was because he had a banana magnet on his giant forehead. Most of the time he wouldn't make it to school that way because he and Bus Driver had some sort of secret pact. If he saw it, he'd always stop and say, "Got another magnet on your head."

Then some certain four-letter words would proceed.

I know it was a mean, cruel thing to do, but have you ever seen fruit on someone's forehead? It's actually really funny.

One Saturday while the Cowboys were playing on TV, I decided to play the magnet game. Before I could situate the magnets perfectly, he woke up, realized what I was doing and started chasing me out of his room. We ran through the kitchen and into the living room. On his way, he grabbed a wooden spoon and began whacking the crap out of my back.

In this house, the one thing we knew was to never disrupt, get in front of, talk over, or even think about messing up the TV while the Cowboys were on. It was Mom's sacred time. Well, sure enough, one swing of the wooden spoon made contact with the satellite receiver and knocked it to a different channel at a crucial point of the game.

I had already run into the other room with Brother following pretty close behind, when I heard a thud and saw him flying straight to the ground. In her anger at us, Mom had thrown the first thing she found on the floor—a tattered, yellow tennis ball. The force of the ball had hit him on the left temple where the metal plate started. Since this was such a sensitive part so near his brain, he had to be careful; any blunt force could cause brain damage or even death.

When I looked down at him after the fall, he was shaking from head to toe, and his eyes were drawn back into his head. I thought he had gotten over his anger at me and was making a joke at Mom's attempt to discipline us, so I started laughing uncontrollably. But Mom wasn't laughing and actually looked quite serious as she ran to Brother as fast as she could. It looked like she was grabbing his tongue and squeezing him. After a few seconds, the shaking stopped and he just looked around like he didn't have any idea what was going on or what had happened.

Mom made him lay down for the next few hours, and I guess that jogged his memory. When he got up, he came over to where I was playing video games and slapped me with that same wooden spoon.

"Now we're even."

I didn't want to start another episode of that, so I simply said, "Fair enough."

And things were back to normal.

Breaking and Entering

A few months later, after one of our special trampoline meetings, Brother, myself and a friend of ours decided to stay the entire night on the trampoline. To me the plan was just to sleep out there, like a campout, but they had much bigger plans. Brother told me that, in order to stay the night outside with them, I would have to do whatever they did. No matter what. So I then became a part of the plan too.

There was an automotive repair shop right across the street, run by a scruffy old drunk we called Jim Bob. Maybe the two teeth he had in his mouth kept him from speaking in an audible tongue, or maybe the fact that he was just crazy made it impossible to understand anything he ever said.

We waited for a few hours after all the lights went out in the house next door to the shop. It was Jim Bob's house, so we knew we would have our chance when those lights were gone. We crossed the street to the right side of the shop building, opposite from his house, and stopped near a side door. There was a window right above the door handle; before I could even turn the knob, I heard a loud crashing of glass amidst the night silence. The sound contrasted like black on white, so we just knew that we were going to get caught. We stayed still for minutes as the feeling passed. Luckily, no one had heard the sound, and soon after, Brother stuck his hand through the break and unlocked the door.

Inside the store portion of Jim Bob's shop, you could buy cigarettes, candy, chips or cokes—the four main food groups, as far as we were concerned. I started piling candy bars into a plastic bag, thinking I had just hit the jackpot. Brother was doing the same with the different cartons of cigarettes, his bag being quite a bit bigger than mine. Then on to the cash register! There were very few actual bills inside, but there was enough change to fill an entire piggy bank jar. We loaded all this change into an oversized Ziploc bag, and as quickly as we had gotten in, we were outside, running back to the trampoline.

We knew better than to stay under the moonlight to count our winnings, so we put all the bags into a big box we had underneath the netting of the trampoline, then rushed inside with it. When we got there, I started counting how many candy bars I had--there were over fifteen! I was instantly ready to start my sugar rush. Brother counted up the change a few minutes later and finally came to the number twenty-seven. We had a ton of candy, twenty-seven bucks in change, and about four cartons of cigarettes.

As we started to divvy up the winnings, I was shut down, given two candy bars and told to get out. I threatened to tell what they did if he didn't share evenly what we had stolen, but then I realized if I told on them, I would be in just as much trouble! I was fighting a battle I would lose, so matter which side I swung for. Since I never told and they never got caught, we (as an uneven team) never got in trouble.

This was just the beginning of my thieving days.

Late Night Star Trek

The best part about the weekends were the TV shows.

In the mornings, I would wake up to cartoons that would last until lunchtime. Then movie marathons until it was dark. And then my favorite part--Twilight Zone and Star Trek until the early hours of the next morning.

By this time we were getting high pretty regularly. Sometimes we would steal the weed Mom kept in her bottom dresser drawer, and if that were combed dry, we would find different aerosol sprays to inhale.

On this particular night, we had found a fabric starch spray that would give you a very weird, funny buzz; we laughed at the most stupid parts of the shows we were watching! Stepdad was away with work again, so we could freely do this without the anxiety of being caught by anyone. I hadn't seen Mom for most of the day. She had been in her room since I woke up—sleeping off a drunken stupor, I guessed. It was good for us though, because she wasn't getting along with any of us the day before. We were having the time of our lives, oblivious to what was being conspired against us in the next room.

All of a sudden, our front door busted open, and Aunt and Granny's Sister flew in like lightning in a storm. I guess, with such haste, they didn't even notice the plastic bags everywhere that we had been huffing from. Or maybe they just knew our house was always a wreck so it didn't faze them. Granny's Sister told us to get outside and get in the car with such a tone that we knew better than to try and defy her. We all went willingly, yet clumsily, to the car, trying not to openly show our impairments.

On the way out, we heard Aunt yelling in Mom's room and Mom crying. I couldn't help my curiosity, so I peered in the door and saw a very familiar, haunting image— Mom, with those same sunken, dark eyes, in almost the same position on the bed, holding that same familiar rifle that kept coming back into my life. My chest immediately sank. I felt I was going to get sick. I held my composure on the outside, but my brain was moving so quickly that I couldn't even answer the basic small talk questions being asked by Granny's Sister.

My brothers just chalked it up to me not being able to conceal my buzz from the spray, but that had passed a long time ago. The only question I could get out was to ask where we were going.

When I was told, "Somewhere safe," I had a pretty good clue as to what Mom had been planning to have happen to all of us that night.

An Average Day

Since the night Mom had introduced me to marijuana, I was hooked. At first I would just go out there once a week at the most, but as the years went by and I got older, it became more abundant. Almost all the friends I had now smoked pot, so someone always had a supply.

The routine was to wake up, get high and go to school until lunchtime. When you're a stoner, one thing you learn is to never turn down a free meal, even if it means having to endure a few hours of school. By the time lunch came around, we were usually coming down from the morning high—and starving.

The next plan on the agenda was the walk back for naptime. This consisted of smoking a joint as we walked through the wooded area leading straight to my backyard. We had a huge couch that sunk down until it was mere inches from the floor as it embraced every portion of your sitting body. After about half a cartoon or a few music videos, we were all out, sleeping as soundly as babies in the womb.

The couple hours of hibernation were enough to have us on the food prowl as soon as our eyes opened back up. Stepdad worked for the HyTop Company now, so our deep freeze was always full of ninety-nine cent microwave pizzas. We would each devour about three of those, then it was off to the streets again to smoke some more. How we never got caught smoking in plain daylight on almost every street in town still amazes me. Our theory was to think of the last place cops would expect to find drugs—to us that meant in plain sight!

Somehow it worked.

look directly at the camera...
no... ok... that works too

We had a rich friend who had all the newest video games, so our next trek would be to his house to get sucked into that realm for a few hours, snacking on chips and Little Debbies. By this time it was getting dark, so we made the journey back home, smoking our nighttime fix, then relaxing to some obscure movie or TV show. Dinner would either be more pizzas, or on rare occasions, Mom made Hamburger Helper slopped in grease and goop. This would be the end of a typical day, flowing into the beginning of a new one where we would follow the exact same steps.

Consistency.

Bad Halloween

It started off like many other events in my life—I just wanted to fit in.

My brothers would only allow this if I did exactly what they wanted me to, or if I did exactly what they were doing. Even if it was against my better judgment.

It was the Halloween after my tenth birthday, and Brother had just bought a pellet gun. We started off to their secret hideout, deep in the woods close to the old football field. After about sixty yards, we came upon a giant, two-story, wooden barn.

There were all sorts of ancient rusted tools and pulleys in the stables, but no animals. On the backside, there was a cracked ladder built into the side of the wooden wall. As we climbed up, one of the rungs gave out and started to crack down the middle, making me almost fall off. With Brother and his friend laughing, I had to play it off like it was funny too.

When we got to the top, there were completely flat hardwood floors, aged and damaged, but still sturdy. They began shooting at birds from the top lookout facing the backside of the barn. I was cold and afraid to even touch the gun, so I just sat there freezing. Brother's Friend called me a baby and handed me a fuzz-filled blanket that was in the corner, covered in dust and gray cobwebs.

As I sat there, trying to get warm, they finally ran out of pellets and began feeling the coldness from sitting still and doing nothing that I had felt the whole time. Brother had the great idea of starting a little fire to keep warm. He had a tiny bottle of lighter fluid in his jacket that he used to refill his Zippo, so he poured a medium-sized circle on the hardwood floors around us. This idea seemed good in theory, and for the next fifteen minutes, it did keep us warm.

We decided that the barn was getting kind of boring, so we decided to head back to the house and get ready for Trick or Treating. Brother knew that if you smothered a flame, it would be put out, so he grabbed the fuzzy, cobweb-and-dust-filled blanket, laid it across the top of the fire and did a few stomps on top. We were already climbing down the wooden ladder; looking up, all I could see was smoke and hear Brother coughing. He said he put it out, but it was just really smoky. Trusting Brother, we all just walked back home and got dressed for Halloween. (I was the Terminator and they just had dumb scary masks they found at the Dollar Store.)

As we started walking to our first house, we heard the sound of sirens zoom past us that weren't the normal police or ambulance sirens. We looked—there was the hardly-ever-used local fire truck sweeping past. We knew it was a big deal if they brought that out. This town was so small that hardly anything ever happened. We were hoping it was the school that had caught on fire, but later found out there was no such luck. As the thrill passed and the excitement of free candy overtook those feelings, we marched up and down every street in town until we had an entire trash bag full of goodies. We ate until we passed out.

When the morning came, we decided to head back to the hideout again. I could eat candy while they shot at birds, making it less boring for me. When we got close to the spot, we heard voices and commotion. It was cops and local officials with badges, standing in front of the barn. Except there was no barn now—it was a pile of black ashes that covered a space about the size of a tennis court. The barn had burned completely to the ground.

As soon as the men saw us, they began asking questions about what we were doing there. Brother, thinking quick, said that we were playing at the football field nearby and decided to explore the woods. They asked us our names and addresses, then told us to be on our way.

A few days later those same people came to our house, asking us questions about the barn that used to be there. I was told to say "nothing about nothing" before I went in. Me being the last to go, of course I ruined it for everyone. At first I told them that I had never been to the barn and knew nothing about it. Then a lady began to tell me that if I was lying, I could go away for a long, long time; if I told her the truth right then, I could save myself from that. Being ten years old, I didn't know she was using scare tactics on me, so I spilled my guts. I told her everything. I was crying, telling her it was an accident, and she thanked me for my honesty.

A few weeks later, we all had to go to the courthouse and sit in front of a real judge. It was one of the most nervous feelings I had ever had. After scolding us for about an hour, he finally told us our sentence. We would be put on juvenile probation for two years, giving us an 8 pm curfew on weekdays and a 9 pm curfew on weekends. In addition to this, we would have to serve 24 hours of community service and pay $620 in restitution fees.

I thought this seemed a much lighter sentence than going to jail for the rest of my life, so I was actually relieved—my criminal record was tainted but still free!

Dolls

There was a room in my house dedicated only to dolls—weird, creepy, face-painted, porcelain dolls.

But they weren't just dolls to Mom. They were her children and it seemed she knew more about them than she knew about us.

There were over a hundred of them, placed delicately in every spot they could fit throughout the entire room. Some days I would come home and catch her just talking to them...and holding pretty good conversations at that! If I were to move one even an inch, she would know exactly who had been moved and the name of the doll as well.

If only she paid that much attention to her real kids.

Stuff

Stupid ~~Stuff~~ Im Scared Of

THE DARK
CLOWNS
WINDOWS
Dolls
The Star Spangled Banner
Machismo
The world expoding
Being Burried Alive in A small coffin
Getting Shot in the Face
Spiders
Dogs
Snakes
Bugs
Did I say the DARK

this list is still accurate

Crackbaby

Some people get nicknames for things they do as a kid, like Twitch or Runner. Others get them for the way they look, like Chubs or Chicken Legs. I got a nickname because of the way I was born—Crackbaby.

Most people I was in contact with didn't even know my real name; they just called me Crackbaby. I was fine with that. I guess I subconsciously even tried to live up to the name by the things I did. To me, it was just what I liked to do, but to others, it made me weird.

I would be high most of the time when walking around town. If I found something on the ground that looked different or interesting, I would pick it up and hide it away in my pocket. By the end of the day, I would have a huge pocketful of what most people would consider trash; to me, it was art. I had a huge wooden treasure chest that I put everything in, and I saved it for years.

These things would eventually be called "crack" items that I put in my "crack box". There was a certain brand of gum I chewed every single day. We called that "crack gum". I just added the word "crack" to pretty much anything with which I had an obsession.

I had become proud to be Crackbaby.

50

Rabbit Hay

We didn't live on a farm anymore, but that didn't keep us from having farm animals. Half of our backyard was filled with a wooden shed that held cages upon cages of Palomino rabbits.

When asked (in a very similar style as before) whether I wanted to help raise these animals, my answer was completely different—I wanted nothing to do with being responsible in any form. Especially on the days when the rabbits would begin to breed too rapidly or get too big for their cages. I won't go into detail, but all I will say is: rabbit stew.

Gross.

The one good thing about these rabbits was, since they were mostly show rabbits, they were on a special diet of premium hay. This hay, even though it smelled nothing like it, looked to be exactly the same consistency and texture of marijuana. Luckily, the people who were into pot to look cool at parties had no clue how it was really supposed to smell. I would take a big chunk of hay, plus the tiniest bit of a roach (smoked-down potent weed), let it sit overnight to infuse it with the smell, divide it into a bunch of individual baggies, and sell it to unknowing high school kids at outrageous prices.

I thought surely I would only get to do this once, so I sold it to as many people as I could before they smoked it and realized they weren't getting high. I made enough money to buy a lot of real pot and felt pretty proud of myself for thinking up such a scheme. About a week later, one of the people I first sold it to came to me and said they needed to talk. I just knew I was about to have to do some defending or maybe even some fighting.

Again I was wrong, because what he actually wanted to talk to me about was getting double the amount this time. Would I cut him a deal if I sold him a higher quantity?

I used all my strength not to laugh in his face, held my composure like a real businessman, and made him a deal. With Stepdad being about as observant as a log, he never noticed half of his rabbit hay was missing every week.

This was the life.

Space Trip

With the life that I was living, doing the same old crap every single day, I longed for something more. At least something different.

I guess I got what I asked for.

Since we began smoking and getting high all the time, our meetings on the trampoline seemed pointless; they eventually just fizzled out. The only time we would go out there was if we just happened to be home while Stepdad was there.

This one night when I was twelve, I saw Oldest Brother and Mom on the trampoline, but didn't see any smoke. Usually I would have been shooed away or kept out of secrets, but they didn't seem to care that I knew what they were doing. They freely offered me a square piece of paper that fit on my tiny fingertip; they told me to put it on my tongue. I tried it and didn't taste anything at all. It was just like I was eating a piece of trash. I figured it was some kind of weird joke being played on me and started to walk off, but was called back. They said I might want to stay outside on the trampoline and just relax for a few minutes. They said it in such droning, monotone voices that my instincts told me to stay there.

As I lay there, looking at the tree branches towering above me, I began to hear something. It was the wind, but at a volume I had never heard it before. In a worried tone, I asked if they could hear it—their response was just laughter. I could hear it bouncing off the sky like we were in an echo chamber. I was starting to get a little sick at my stomach, even panicky, as things felt like they were starting to move in slow motion. I was told that I needed to calm down; the piece of paper I had put in my mouth was going to give me a whole new level of high.

After about an hour, my body finally got used to the way I was seeing and hearing things. Laughter soon ensued and I was having the time of my life! I felt like a super-hero with superhuman vision and hearing. I found that, the more relaxed I got, the more intense were the things I saw. Not only were there tracers of light following everything that moved, but now there were colors following the tracers.

We went from the trampoline to the old station wagon which, having been broken down for the past few years, was now just a lawn ornament. While we sat inside the car, we started smoking and the clouds began to take the shapes of whatever I was thinking about. The sky outside was so dark that, for a bit, I thought the station wagon was a spaceship floating aimlessly in the atmosphere. It began to rain on the windshield and side windows where I was looking out. To me, the drops were stars and planets we passed on our trip to nowhere.

I'm not sure how long we were in that car, but I know it was a while because I saw the sun's light emerging from somewhere in the rearview mirror. We must have been close to our destination; being this close to the sun must have made the rays that shot from its core a million times more intense than if we had been on Earth. The brightness was too much for my eyes to take, so they slid under the cover of their lids to wait for us to pass.

The next thing I remember was waking up alone in the station wagon with an intense headache. My super powers had faded. We weren't on a new planet. Had it all been a weird dream and I just sleepwalked to the car? That was my guess...until I went inside and saw one of my brothers with a piece of paper the size of a Post-It with about fifty individual squares on it. They all bore a smiley face, just like the one given to me last night.

Acid trip Age 13 ish

This would start a very imaginative part of my life.

Snail eye crayons

Franken-stoned

53

Needing More

brown Sounds

54

Redneck Parties

I don't think you can really say you've been to a party until you go to a party in the country.

You've got to have people there with names like Blue Tick, Jimmy Mac, and Rat Tail Ray; a trailer house in the middle of the woods; a bonfire; a fridge where the only contents are booze and fish bait. This was a setting where some of the most outrageous and off-the-wall things happened.

Girls would get drunk and break bottles on their heads to show they could be tough too. Guys would play Human Darts and a ridiculous game called Dodge the Shotgun. (You can imagine that safety was definitely not an issue here.) One night Blue Tick tripped acid so hard that he thought his body was on fire, began stripping and running around naked in the woods by the trailer, screaming. This soon became known as the Blue Tick Tango and was replicated for laughs at many future parties.

Pretty much, if it could be thought of, it was done.

Satanic Nazis

The influence from your friends can sometimes blind you to the stupidity that you're actually surrounding yourself with. Now, I could never imagine myself doing Satanic rituals or hating someone because of their skin color or religious beliefs. But back then, being submerged in nothing but that had started to consume me.

I had alienated all my friends except for a twenty-two year old, self-proclaimed Satanist and his twenty-six year old Wiccan wife. They seemed much smarter and wiser to me than any of my young, immature friends. They had passion about the things they believed in, to the point where it was made believable. I longed for something or someone to believe in. They taught me the lie of the Aryan race: to hate, despise and not tolerate anything different than myself, whether it was skin color, sexual preference or the god to which they prayed.

I found myself cussing at people from behind the comfort of car windows, under my breath at gas stations and even at school—just for being black, overly Christian, or even for looking "gay". Hatred was consuming me, and it felt good at the time. I felt empowered, like I could do anything I could imagine. Like I could hurt anyone at any moment and feel totally fine about it. This anger led to even darker feelings. I was angry at people for trying to shove their God down my throat, knowing that what I had was far more powerful than the Invisible Man they pled to. I was accepted by this power and these people, so I would do things for them without even thinking.

On this night, they asked if I could get one of Stepdad's bunnies and bring it to the motel down the street where they lived. I grabbed an old, rusty dog carrier used to transport the prize bunnies to and from the shows that seemed so ridiculous to me, and shoved one of the ugly bunnies inside. It kicked a bit and gave me a few scratches, but it didn't even faze me because I knew I was going to be praised by my much older friends for doing a good job.

When I got there, the hotel was much cleaner than it had ever been before, with dark black comforters on the one window that looked outside. There was a black sheet with white paintings on it laid across the entire floor in front of the full size bed. The paintings were of a star encased in a circle with the image of some kind of animal in the middle, horns stretching across the top two points of the upside-down star. At each side of the blanket were four big, reddish-brown rocks, each with a black candle placed on top of it. I handed over the cage; they took the bunny out, broke its legs so it wouldn't run off, and laid it on the sheet.

This flashed in front of my eyes and all of a sudden, the hypnotic haze that had been hovering over my brain for the last few months started depleting. It was as if my brain had spilled all of my common sense onto the floor, and now it was finally being vacuumed back inside. I knew what was going to happen next, and I knew I could do nothing to stop it. Just as I saw in my head, it started happening.

They lit all four candles and began speaking so intensely that I could feel my tiny bones shaking my heart around. I sat there for a few minutes, composing my next move so thoroughly, but when I decided to do something, I forgot my original plan and just ran screaming for the door. As I did, all four candles extinguished them-selves at once and a darkness more black than the deepest hole on earth took over. There were sounds so loud and piercing that I had to hold my ears on the two or three running steps to the door. When I got there, I frantically jiggled all the locks and tried to open the door, but to no avail. It was as if it were a sealed-up tomb. The fear took me over to the point where I was just slamming my feeble body into the door repeatedly, screaming and crying at the top of my lungs.

The few seconds that this went on seemed to last for weeks, like a bad dream in which you never wake up. Then the door finally came open, and the daylight broke through as I took one last glance back to see the people I had admired for so long in a totally different way.

They were weak, lying face first next to a disturbing mess of what used to be a helpless bunny. I started to throw up in the parking lot, sick at what I saw and sick at myself for being a part of it. I ran back toward my house crying, thinking, pleading to be free from the way I felt. I didn't really know to Whom I was pleading, since I had tried both sides and still felt nothing; it was more of a plea to anyone or anything.

I stayed in a weird, depressed state for about a week, thinking about my life, staying in my room, and not going out of the house. Finally, I broke down and decided to go back to the motel. When I got there, the door was open and a lady was cleaning inside. Everything was gone except for the bed, and as I asked where the tenants were, she began to tell me in broken English.

"Cops came. Lady fight. Drive them away."

What I finally found out was, a few days after the incident, they had gotten in a fight that ended with them stabbing each other. When the cops came, they found that both had outstanding warrants for their arrests, so they were put in a jail for the next few years.

I didn't know it, but my pleas to Whomever had been answered.

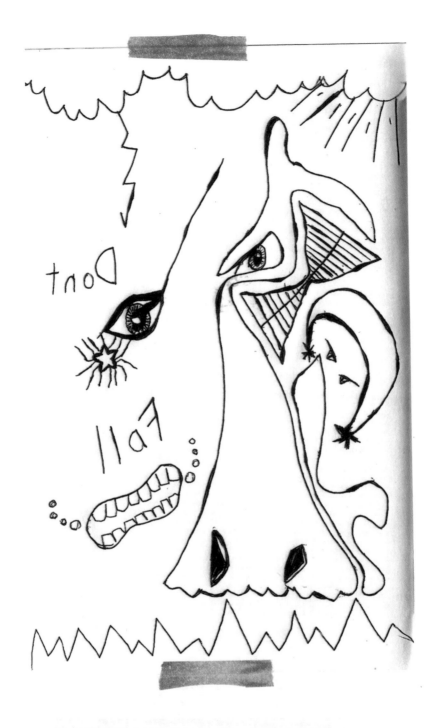

dont fall just breath

People who try to act macho
are ~~goofy~~ ignorant. I MEAN
where is the porpose in pretending
to be something just so people
will think your MANLY. ~~xxxxx~~
I think you should be who you
are and if someone doesnt Like
you for it ~~xxxx~~. I dont
try to be anything but people
get the impression that im trying
to be different. well If they
want to think that just because
I dont follow the crowd and
think and act like the people who
are pretending AND HIDING UNDER
Tommy Hillfigger ~~xxxx~~ that
I am different or "weird" beeuz
of it then let them. It doesnt
bother. me im the one who sees
the world clearly. not in a blurry
Haze of fashion AND morals.

my stoned journal/entrys & drawings

Tim Frost
November 12, 2014

Driving this kid to school today I started thinking back at what I was doing in 7th grade. The grade that also happened to be my last year I would ever go to school, I was smoking pot, hanging out with racist satanist, and doing more drugs than my 13 year old body should have been able to handle. I can't even wrap my mind around the idea of O doing anything close to that yet as a kid I thought everything was perfectly normal.

It was a huge reminder of redemption and the hope that anyone's story can be broken from past lies and hurts. No one is predestined for failure. The mistakes that I've made in my past I hold no regrets for because in the mistakes is where healing and learning take place. I've learned how to be a better father and a husband by taking even the mistakes I've made there and communicating why things didn't work and finding a solution for future situations as they come up. It's a continual learning process everyday and I feel so blessed and honored to get to be on this journey.

As my book gets closer and closer to finding it's way to publishers and I'm getting ready to embark on a new season of my life where I'm speaking my story in public, I feel anxious. Vulnerable on the highest level completely exposed to people I know and love and even to strangers who will only know me by my story. I would ask you to pray for our family as this new change occurs that any decisions I make be covered by grace and any mistakes made in the process would just be new learning tools to make

the journey that much more fruitful. Taking a story of darkness and completely washing it with the light of hope and redemption. Love y'all's.

Tag Photo   Add Location   Edit

Like   Comment   Share

View 10 more comments

Cory Dusek I am so convicted after reading this post, I just had to say I'm sorry for helping lead u astray, and labeling u with the name crack baby. Jesus has done a work in my life and I am telling my story as well. I hope u can forgive an old friend and maby one day we can worship The Lord together!!

Write a comment...

Charlie

There was a mystery man in the drug world who we all called Charlie.

The people higher up actually went to see him, to pick up the drugs from his house way out in the piney woods of East Texas. Us lower ranking druggies would either just wait in town for runners to come back with the drugs, or we would go with and get dropped off by a little pond a few miles from Charlie's house. Most of the time I would rather go, that way I knew someone wasn't smoking my weed all the way home without me.

The trip wound through about ten miles of curving country roads until we got to a blacktop. Then it was another two miles before being dropped by a small feeding silo near a shallow pond. Usually the wait was only about ten to fifteen minutes, but other times it took a little longer. It was always an anxious wait with a million things going through your head at once—wondering if they got busted or if Charlie went crazy and killed them or if they ran off the road on the way (however far away it was) to his house. Every time I would begin to worry...then I would see the car zooming around the corner to pick us up and be reassured again.

The first night I actually got to see Charlie was a scary one. Everyone else in the car knew him and had his permission to be in house, but I still didn't. I was dropped off right before sunset and sat Indian-style under the silo, making drawings in the dirt with a broken stick. After a few minutes, I saw the sun hide completely behind the now-darkened skies, and being afraid of the dark, I tried not to worry myself. It seemed every little sound was something coming from deep in the woods to eat me. After a few minutes of pacing in the wooded area, I couldn't take it anymore and headed for the road where it felt safer.

It was taking forever this time and I just knew something was going wrong.

Just like clockwork, when I started to completely freak out, I saw the headlights of a car coming. I stood there, thankful for the human contact heading my way, but as it got closer, my heart started to sink. This was not the car I had come here in—it was a much louder, older, Ford truck. I recognized the passenger as one of the people I drove up with, but not the driver. He was a long-haired, bearded man with yellow teeth, wearing a stained wife-beater, cut-off blue jean shorts and steel-toe work boots. He got out, holding a shotgun, cussing and screaming.

"Who in the hell are you?"

The guy I came with vouched for me, saying I was with him and there was nothing to worry about. He must have asked twenty times if I was a narc; obviously the darkness must have been covering my figure because I was just a kid! (A narc—as in a narcotics officer—is a term stoners use to call people out that snitched on them.) After about five minutes of convincing him I was just a regular kid, the gun was finally aimed away from my face—quite a relief. I've had my fair share of unpleasant shotgun moments. Then, after a stern cussing out by Charlie, I was told to never hide in the woods again when I came up there. He said he wanted to see my face.

He had been doing drugs for a long time, probably before I was even thought of, and it showed. His face sagged, his teeth hung like rotten shingles from his mouth and his skin was as rough as sandpaper. His mind wasn't all there either. We would be outside—me, my brother and Charlie—and he would have Brother convinced that the stars in the sky were really DEA helicopters using infrared satellite cameras to try to take pictures of him. He then proceeded to throw his middle finger up to the sky and scream obscenities until I thought his lungs were going to collapse. Brother would blindly follow, doing the same thing. Then they would both laugh and think they had gotten the best of those helicopter cameramen.

I retained regular visits to Charlie's house over the next year or so until one day, right before we were about to go make a purchase, we got news from one of his other customers. He said that Charlie had lost it and shot at a mutual acquaintance because he thought she was trying to get him busted. We didn't know if we should believe that or not, but just to be on the safe side, we waited a few days.

Sure enough, it was all over the news. There was a drug bust in Hainesville, and Charlie was taken to prison, probably for the rest of his life considering all the drugs and illegal weapons he was hoarding. We had second thoughts about what we were doing with our lives; that only lasted for about a day. We soon found another way to get the same things Charlie offered us and we were back in business.

You would have thought we would have more logic than that, but I guess you really don't think logically if you're on drugs.

School...or the Lack Thereof

School was definitely a different experience for me as I got older. It had become a burden that I hated to attend. My severe lack of respect for people who tried to tell me what to do, coupled with teachers and faculty who didn't understand me made for quite the combo. I had pretty much always done what I wanted, and if anyone or anything kept me from that, there would definitely be problems.

Having moved on to a few different drugs made for a pretty wide range of mood swings. Whether it was coming down from getting high in the morning or from a two-day speed binge, there would always be someone to rub me the wrong direction.

My science teacher in particular seemed to have it in for me. She would always call on me first to answer questions and read out loud in class. My responses were usually just a few select four-letter words that would make the class laugh and get me thrown into the hallway to march to a principal who had no clue what to do with me.

They tried sending me to the alternative school where they let the kids have smoke breaks on the patio every few hours. It seemed that even at the alternative school they didn't want me because after a few months I was sent back to the regular one to finish up the last few weeks. I would have just stayed home like I had been doing, but being on probation, I was constantly being awakened by a truancy officer who would drive me to school whether I was wearing pajamas or clothes that had been on my body for weeks.

A few weeks before the summer break was over, he told me that I had the choice to go to regular school or to a juvenile detention center in Greenville. This made the drudgingly hard task even more of a burden. I went, but was stuck back in the seventh grade again to repeat this horrible experience with absolutely no escape other than going to kid jail.

I tried to make the most of it by getting even higher at school and bringing different toys to play with while I was there.

My usual routine was to get high before school, eat breakfast with my free lunch card, then go back for seconds with Brother's free lunch card. Afterward I would retire for a little nap in the art room, usually waking up right before lunchtime. Outside there was a big dumpster beside the art room that I would hide my joints under to smoke before going to have my two free lunches. When lunch was over, I would grab any of the roaches (hits of weed) I had left, walk past the baseball fields and into the woods, heading home. Teachers and staff started noticing my drugged-up state of mind, I suppose, because I was "asked" to take a mandatory drug test. Mom didn't like the fact that the school was calling me a druggie, so she went up and gave them a piece of her mind.

There was a plethora of old Dr. Pepper memorabilia in Principal's office. Bottles, glass plaques and tins lined the desk and shelves. As I stayed on the wooden bench outside of the office, I could hear Mom's voice starting to get louder and more defensive through the glass window. I got up and peeked inside to hear her cussing, telling him that we didn't need his "shitty judgmental school". I could hear fear rising in Principal's voice as he tried, to no avail, to calm her. She began slinging her arms like a wild horse shaking his head around, knocking tons of the priceless items to the ground, shattering them. She was on a rampage, going from windowsill to countertop, cussing and screaming the entire time.

By this point, Principal was on the phone to someone; we realized a few minutes later that it was the police. Two people grabbed Mom's arms and asked her to leave. Right as she started to resist, we saw a cop through the window and Mom said, "We are leaving and don't you ever think I will be bringing my son back to such a shitty, accusatory place!"

We walked out the backdoor with the two people who had been restraining Mom walking behind to make sure we got out. Mom was yelling at them and making a scene in front of all the students and staff as we left. This would be my last day of school at twelve years of age.

Later that day I heard Mom on the phone with a homeschool salesman. As he told her how much it cost, she asked, "How old do you have to be to legally quit school? Sixteen? Okay Tim, if anyone asks, from now on you're sixteen. Thank you! Bye."

Being sixteen for almost four years gets really, really confusing.

getting stoned, pretending i could drive
AGE 11/6"

Bleach

I don't mind cleaning, but there is one smell I still cannot take.

Bleach.

It's forever burned in my nostrils as something that makes my stomach curdle. I've tried using it as much as I can to get over this sensation, but nothing has ever worked.

It all started one night while two Brothers were at their dad's in Ft. Worth and Oldest Brother was at his job at the local park. It was just Mom and me alone while I played video games and she did some cleaning—very rare for her. Our house was always completely disgusting. Moldy dishes in every room, rotten fruit with flies circling it in the kitchen, cockroaches everywhere. If you went into the kitchen at night and turned on the light, the probability that you would see even an inch of actual floor not covered in roaches was one in a billion. They crunched and cracked as you walked through to the refrigerator. We were so used to them that it really wasn't even a big deal to us anymore. If they got on a slice of pizza that had been left out, I would just shake them off and keep eating.

Needless to say, pretty disgusting.

After finishing up my hours of Super Mario, I went to the restroom for a much-needed bathroom break. As I walked through the house, the smell of cleaners got stronger and stronger. I saw the bathroom door closed and heard the sound of the shower going. There was steam coming through the crack underneath the door as I knocked to see how much longer Mom would be in there. I didn't get a reply, so I knocked harder and spoke louder.

Still nothing.

By this time I was yelling and banging as hard as I could, knowing from past experiences that it was not a good sign for Mom to be locked in any room and not responding. "I'm going to break in if you don't answer me!"

That being my last straw, I began keying the lock with a safety pin and a paperclip. (Having brothers who purposely stayed in the bathroom longer than they needed just to make me mad, I learned ways to get in.) As I opened the door slowly, hoping not to see Mom naked, I saw an image even worse—she was slumped facedown by the bathtub and there were about nine empty bleach bottles thrown across the floor. The stench from the bleach and the steam from the shower making it rise almost made me throw up. It was definitely hard to breath and there was no telling how long Mom had been inside. I tried to move her, wake her up, but it was not working at all. Her face was a pale sheet of white and her lips were turning a light grayish-blue color.

Crying, I ran out to the phone, but I guess no one had paid the bill because there was no dial tone. As I ran outside to use a neighbor's phone, I saw Oldest Brother drive up and frantically told him the situation. He went in, grabbed Mom up, clumsily staggered outside and put her into his car. I tried to get in but was told to stay at the house. He drove as quickly as he could to the hospital a few blocks away.

I must have been in shock because everything around was going in slow motion. The next thing I remember is falling slowly to the ground, hitting my head on a box of cassette tapes. What seemed like a few minutes later, I awoke, bleach still stagnate in the air, and walked clumsily to the door as Granny entered. She took me in her arms, laid me down on the couch away from the smell and told me it was ok, that I needed to rest. I slept the rest of the night without waking once. When morning came, I saw Mom in her own bed, sleeping just as soundly as I had.

After a few days she was back to her old normal self. Nothing was ever said about the bleach incident or why it happened.

Brother VS Cop

Oldest Brother had a girlfriend when he got older that he couldn't seem to keep. This also seemed to wildly alter his moods. If they were doing good, he would come home as happy as he could be, but on the flip side, there were times I thought he had lost part of his mind. Breaking things and slamming doors were a good sign that things were not going to be happy and cheery that night.

This particular night was more confusing than any of them though. He came in as weak as if he had been in a brutal fight, pummeled by his opponent. No doors were slammed; they were barely even opened as he almost crawled into his room. The door closed slowly behind him and we all knew to not even think about going in there.

A few hours passed and Stepdad was calling us into the kitchen for some concoction he had whipped up from the scraps left floating in the fridge. Oldest Brother didn't come, so Stepdad went into his room to get him.

With his unobservant eyes, he didn't see Brother at first, but then nearly stepped on his hand as he was walking through. Brother was lying on the floor next to an emptied bottle of aspirin. I had taken a ton of those before, trying to get high, and nothing ever happened, so I wondered what his plan was. He was conscious with his eyes open, so I don't know how the pills were affecting him at that moment, but he got up and ran for his dresser. There was a knife on top that he grabbed and started to go for his wrist. Stepdad stopped his hand inches before he reached skin contact; the force knocked the knife to the floor. He quickly kicked the knife to the other room before Brother could reach for it again. He yelled at Stepdad, "I'm going to KILL you if you don't let me go!" but Stepdad had a firm position on top of Brother's chest. Finally he kicked loose and ran to my room.

Stepdad went to the phone and called the cops. (I guess he had taken enough of this and thought it would be the last straw.) By this time Oldest Brother had crawled into the attic and was hiding--shaking, scared, and confused.

When the cops got to the house, they yelled for him to come down from the attic. He refused, so they used force and ended up pulling him down. He hit the ground near my toy boxes with a thud as I watched it all from the top bunk bed. I guess that this made him even angrier, because soon an all-out brawl had started in the floor beside my bed. They blocked all his efforts to attack them except one—a swift blow from Brother's fist to the left side of the cop's face. After that, all I saw was him being thrown on his face and his hands coming behind his back in cuffs. They marched him straight out to their police car and were gone within minutes.

He pled not guilty. The only person who saw the entire thing was me, and I didn't tell anyone that I saw anything. He ended up only having to go to a mental rehabilitation center for a little over a week, and pay some court fees and other fines, I think. When he came back, he seemed to have his stuff together...at least on the outside.

The Slap

I don't know if it was because of the full moon or some other unnatural force, but tensions were at an all-time high in the house tonight.

I was angry at Mom for spending one of the few child support checks I got from my real dad on alcohol. Stepdad had been gone with work for the past few weeks, so that meant no one went to the grocery store. With us and all of our friends getting high and snacking, our food supply had drained to the bare minimum of apple juice and a few cans of corn. I usually wouldn't have the guts to confront Mom face to face, but I was so angry that I didn't care. This made both of our moods even worse as we started yelling and cussing at each other.

"If your brain wasn't so screwed up, you wouldn't need to drink to cope!"

She responded with words that enraged me to the point of breaking. "If I didn't hate you so much, I wouldn't need to drink!"

My blood began pumping through my body so intensely that I could feel the heat radiating off of me! Involuntarily, I pulled my hand up and swung it as hard as I could across Mom's face.

Silence ensued and I knew I was in the eye of a fast moving hurricane of rage soon to sweep over my entire being. Everything was in slow motion. Then it hit—Mom's wrath coming at me full force in all its anger, driving swings across the top of my head as I ducked and tried to retreat. After a few seconds of this, I felt my entire body lift off the ground as Mom took me by my shirt and hurled me out the door, screaming, "BYE!!!! And don't even THINK of coming back!"

I had no intention to, but also had no clue where I would go. Being thirteen, my prospects didn't look good, but I knew some friends who would let me crash with them for a bit. I wasn't sure exactly what would happen if I tried to go back home, but for the time being, I would let that remain a mystery.

every feeling summed into one picture

CHAPTER FOUR
The Shuffle

Caught on Fire

Well, by now you could have guessed that fire and I didn't have the best of interactions. Maybe it was just my accident-prone mentality or mere stupidity, but I was at it again.

After I left my house, I stayed with Oldest Brother in a trailer a few blocks down the road, hidden from the main highway. I had become friends with a lot of potheads and dealers by now, so I was always well stocked with weed and the occasional hits of acid. This was probably the main reason Brother didn't mind me staying around.

One night, we all got really high while eating Teddy Grahams and watching cable TV on this old clunker TV that Granny gave me. It was winter and the trailer didn't have very good heating, so each room was equipped with an electric heater. My room, the living room, had a four-foot wide electric heater with metal grating along the side of it. The inside glowed a neon orange color, emitting enough heat to make the entire room pretty toasty when put on high.

I fell asleep in an old maroon sleeping bag on the floor next to the warmth of the heater. The next thing I saw was smoke all around my sleep-filled eyes; I started coughing. My first guess was that someone had failed at an attempt to make cookies again, but what I saw next made me know I was dead wrong—fire   coming from the bottom half of my body. My sleeping bag had caught on fire!

No sooner had I noticed it, than Brother came in and started laughing, "Oh crap... you're on fire!!!! Roll around!!" As I rolled around on the floor, struggling to get control of both legs that had fallen asleep, I could hear Brother still laughing as he ran to the sink. This was not funny at all to me. It felt like a bad dream when someone is chasing you, but you have no control over any part of your body; you're just frozen still.

I finally managed to scoot out of the bag using my chest and hand muscles, only to be greeted with a cold splash of water over my entire body. The flames were out and all that was left was a thick layer of smoke and stench lying across the room. With the lights now on, we opened the front and back sliding doors of the trailer to let out the smoke and assessed the damage. The flames never made it through the thick padding of the sleeping bag, so I was not burned at all. There were just a few matted burns in the carpet about the size of a basketball from my rolling around, as well as a huge line of maroon melted on the grates of the heater.

Being soaking wet with huge drafts of cold air coming in through the doors was not my idea of something funny either, but all of this was hysterical to Brother. I borrowed some wind pants with a drawstring waist and one of his oversized t-shirts to wear through the night until I could sneak back to the house to get some of my dry clothes. Since the heater was toast, I put my black hoodie back on and found an extra blanket to fall asleep with on the couch.

I had become a joke that would last for years, anytime someone would come over and ask how those burn marks got in the carpet. At first it was annoying to have people mocking and making fun, but eventually (after a few joints) I would be laughing and recreating the scene turn by turn. It is amazing how far a little mindless self-indulgence can go.

Music

Living with my Older Two in Arlington was almost like a daydream it was so quick. It's where I first remember being truly inspired to be a musician.

Half Sister had gotten all of us tickets to a concert that I could never even say the name of...Lolla-pop-looza? The main reason I wanted to go was to see my favorite band—Nirvana. Theirs was the first tape I remember buying at Walmart. I recall popping it in the tape player of Mom's blue station wagon, seeing her disgust as the grunge blared out.

I was in love.

The tickets were a birthday present, but the concert wasn't until the first of August. In April we were sitting around the big-screen TV, watching music videos, when a newsbreak popped up announcing they had found Kurt Cobain's dead body in his garden house in Seattle.

A little extra "seasoning" with our turkey in this meal

I couldn't believe it—this was my hero, one of my musical idols! It felt like a family member dying.

I had to tuck that sadness inside like everything else because my brothers had just let it flake off their shoulders like snow. If I started crying or acting sad, I would lose any amount of cool that I might've had. It really affected me though. I lost all interest in going to the concert that previously felt like I had waited my whole life for. I decided against going and just stayed home while my brothers and their friends went. When they got back, I knew I had made a mistake because of how they talked it up as one of the most amazing things they had ever done.

I waited all year for tickets to go on sale again. This time I decided, no matter who was playing, I would be there.

Beatdown

Even when I lived with my brothers, I still ended up couch surfing and staying other places for weeks at a time. This time it was with my friends that became like a new family—I even began to care about them more than my biological one. We'd laugh together, cry together, take care of each other, get mad and make up together. I remember a night when the Fam went for a drive on the outskirts of Dallas to a big cow pasture...

We all got out and were on a shroom hunt, each with our own black trash bag rustling behind us as we ran. Within about twenty minutes or so, we all had pretty good lumps of the poop-flaked mushrooms in each bag and were heading to a party with some friends, as well as people we had never seen before and probably never would again.

I was sitting in the back with a girl we called Lass. She had blonde hair with a couple of purple streaks wisping through her bangs and a style all her own. We always had a special connection; I was scared to ever make a move for fear I would ruin that special relationship. She was my bestie. I was there for her when guys dumped her, and when she decided it was time to ditch them herself. She smoked a lot of pot with me, but she had never done shrooms before. She decided to try them out this night. She didn't like the fact that she was going to be chewing on something that came from cow crap, so I cleaned them off for her and diced them into small, pill-like pieces so she could just swallow them.

About twenty minutes later I started to regret giving them to her. She had a low tolerance to most drugs as it was, and she ended up taking more shrooms than I thought. She was also drinking, which I didn't realize would have such an effect when mixed with shrooms since I didn't ever drink. Soon she was in a corner, trying to pile clouds on her face one minute and crying the next. By that time, I was starting to feel it, looking round at all the different people in the room. There were about twenty; ten I knew, others I had seen around, but a few, never in my life.

I had been keeping my eyes on Lass throughout the night, but I lost her after a few hours. As I went looking around in each room of the trailer house, I finally saw her. My blood started to boil, and my heart was beating so fast. The rage of a million bees felt like it was buzzing in my brain.

She was in a back bedroom on a love seat, almost completely lifeless save her few futile attempts to bat this guy's hands away from her. He had taken her jeans and pulled them down, and was trying to make his way up her shirt. She was telling him to stop, but with the state she was in, she could barely even curve her lips into audible sound.

With all my rage, I ran and began kicking and screaming like a sailor in a bar, relishing every ounce of pain I was inducing on this guy's chest. After about six good kicks, I began hitting his face with fists clenched so tight, they could've broken ice. My friends were soon at my back, trying to pull me off, not knowing the situation. As soon as they realized what I was screaming and Lass' current state, the Family Protection Gene kicked in. They all started taking their turns, releasing their frustration. It seemed like this went on for hours, but I knew it was just a fleeting few moments until the guy was lying on the floor in his underwear and socks. We knew that if we kept hitting him, it could end very badly, so there was a voice of reason that made us stop.

At that moment, Lass' real older brother walked in. His eyes were completely mad when he realized what was going on, but there were no fists thrown. He picked the guy up and chunked him in his car; a few of us got in with him. The girls stayed back with a few guys to comfort Lass and let her get some rest. We drove for about thirty minutes until we came to a pretty shady neighborhood, where we stopped with the car still running. Lass' brother threw the guy in the street. He started honking the horn and screaming at the top of his lungs until the entire neighborhood was aware of us, then we sped off.

Leaving the guy in that neighborhood, his body half-naked, didn't really make sense until I got a little older. I still don't know what happened to him that night, but I did know one thing for sure: No one messes with the Family.

Bad Meat

After being back with Brother again, he got tired of me always mooching off him and he said it was time for me to go. Where to next? Back to East Texas, I guess.

I had a friend named Joshie who lived in a trailer house on the back part of a wood shop that made different kinds of furniture. It was owned by his family, so he pretty much got to do whatever he wanted back there. Originally I was only going to stay a few nights, but my few nights turned into more of a permanent residence. We would stay up all night playing bass and guitar outside as loud as we wanted, not giving a care about anything.

One night we decided to make some hamburger meat for supper...since that's all we had. We looked around the house and the only two things we found to go with it were mustard and ketchup, so I took one and he took the other. There should have been a warning light go off in my head, because I had seen the meat sitting on the kitchen counter two days ago, and now we were cooking with it. We just figured we'd cook the germs off. A few minutes later, we were drowning one bowl of meat with ketchup and the other with mustard and eating like we hadn't done so in weeks. It actually wasn't that bad when you added a little extra salt to it.

We sat down on the floor and started watching The Wonder Years on TV. In the middle of the first episode, I started feeling really thirsty. I got up and started to walk outside to the Coke machine where we knew a trick to get free Pepsis, but didn't make it past the kitchen. My entire body felt like I had been on a merry-go-round for days, then I just fell over face first on the rotting linoleum kitchen floor.

That was about 9 pm; the next thing I remember was the sun coming through the cracks underneath the bent-back metal on the bottom of the front door. I had been passed out all night and still felt a little dizzy as I walked back to the bedroom.

blast off indeed...

Joshie was laid out on the floor with a Nintendo controller draped across his body. The meat had turned us into zombies; every move we tried to make felt impossible. This was worse than any bad drug trip that I had ever had before.

We decided, from that day on, to just hold out if we were ever that hungry again.

Video Games

One thing I considered myself better at than most people was video gaming. I probably played more hours of games than I actually went to school. There wasn't one I couldn't beat—blindfolded, with both hands tied behind my back, in the dark while half asleep. I mean, it was second nature. Mostly due to skipping school so much to just get high and play all day.

I would get excited when I saw commercials of new games that were coming out, and begin plotting ways to get them. I remember this one time; I grabbed a tea pitcher and taped a sheet of paper to the side of it that said "Please Donate". I went around the entire town and asked for donations for a fake Little Dribblers basketball team I called "The Flyers". I ended up collecting over fifty bucks, and had Mom drive me to the Walmart to pick out my new game prize. It was almost too easy.

Well, there was a new game coming out that I kept seeing the commercial for, but I didn't even have the system to play it, so it seemed it would just be a dream. My cousin was staying with Granny; he said he thought he might have a way to raise the money to get the game AND the system. There was a safe inside Granny's house that only locked with one deadbolt and he knew where the key was hidden. I just knew that Granny would notice if we were to take any money out of the safe because there were mostly just documents and extra keys inside. However, after getting high, all rational thought was thrown out the window and we were so worried about the video game that we weren't going to let anything stop us.

Wednesday was the day that the old ladies from the nursing home came to the ceramic shop to paint and glaze things, so we knew Granny would be nowhere near the house for a while. We found the key and began digging throughout the metal safe built into the wall behind the door. After minutes of looking with no luck, we finally found an envelope that said "Christmas" on it. Inside was a one hundred dollar bill and two twenties curled underneath it. With the nine dollars we had between the both of us and our newly acquired one hundred and forty dollars, we had reached our goal.

We went to Walmart and bought exactly what we had been waiting for—going home to play for hours after getting high. I felt bad about stealing from Granny every now and then, but would abruptly shut it down by a puff of smoke or a hit of acid.

I found out much later how Granny had been saving that money to buy a $10 Christmas toy for each one of her fourteen grandchildren. She beat herself up about losing that money for a long time, but never once suspected me or Cousin of taking it.

That would hold a shadow over my mind for a long time.

Granny and Laughter

To this day, I still never told my Granny we stole that money. Maybe today I could call her up and tell her it was us. She did the best she could to help raise us 4 boys when mom was not well enough to do so. I am thankful for her presence in our lives, and feel like a lot of my humor and quirkiness I can attribute to her. The relationship we have now consists of random prank calls that I make to her, insisting she just won 2 free tickets to Heaven. She gets so riled up it that I just know cuss words will be flying thru the phone at any time.

Granny: "I do not need tickets! Jesus paid for my tickets with his blood on the cross!"

Me: "But do you know where are your seats located, m'am? We have the best seats in the house."

Granny: "MY SEATS ARE RIGHT NEAR THE THRONE!" *long silence broken by my slight snicker* "TIMOTHY! I'M GOING TO COME DOWN THERE AND SPANK YOU!"

Then full on laughter ensues and we finish up with a quasi-normal conversation.

So, the laughter. Laughter has always been a heavy warm blanket that I used to cover raw hurtful emotions. Even when laughter wasn't appropriate, it helped me navigate the dark waters. It was learned and passed down thru the family tree, to a fault. There's healthy humor and then there's the kind used to cover the uncomfortable or the painful. That was our forte'. Got something difficult to talk about? Just say it really loud like it is a joke and boom—you are done. You said the thing, and you are all laughing so you don't have to deal with the fall-out.

Over the years I've learned to balance the healthy and not-so-healthy humor but it has definitely been a challenge. When you've spent years covering up hurts with dark humor it's hard to actually feel pain and sit in that brokenness. I have learned the healing that comes after actually dealing with pain is where a lot of my growth has come from. Now, I try to laugh when laughing is really real and hurt when I need to hurt...which hurts. And that sucks. But those laughs with granny...those are just healthy healing laughs and I'm thankful for those.

Where's My Stuff

Ever so often I would need to go back to my storage house (otherwise known as Mom's house) to get extra clothes or things that were too big to fit in the suitcase/backpack that was attached to my body. (It was like an extra limb.)

This one time in particular, I was making my way to the front door when I saw a beat-up old Chevy backed completely up to the door. I didn't make anything of it until I got my way around and inside; I saw that over half of Mom's junk was missing from the house, simultaneously being loaded in the bed of this truck. I looked around but didn't see Mom, only some of her homely best friends in grease-stained, pearl-snapped shirts instead, wandering around like roaches. They were grabbing boxes of hoarded goods that my parents had won from auctions or garage sales, sorting them onto the truck. I asked what was going on and they simply told me that my parents had moved to a town called Linden. They would be here within the hour for another load.

Not that I cared at the time, but looking back, I guess it's kind of weird to move to a town two hours away without inviting your thirteen year old son.

I waited around, looking for any of my stuff I could find, when I came upon a box that just had "Timmie's Shit" written on the side in permanent marker (Probably one of my brother's doings). Sure enough, that's what it was—a collection of things that mattered to me and only me, along with a small, grey vintage suitcase that had some of my clothes in it.

Within a half hour or so, Mom came walking through the door as if nothing strange at all was going on. I said, "Oh, you moved, huh?"

always a gamer

me and granny eventually
reconciled — early 2000's

"Oh yeah. Haha...did you want to come with us?" She kind of half-said under her breath, anticipating the answer before I could even speak.

"Nah. I'm fine," was my response and I actually believed it...and was even relieved she would be so much further away.

"Well, I left a box for you in your old bedroom. It was everything I found that looked weird enough to be yours."

"Oh, I found it," I said, with a kind of a half-laugh, as if I was responding to her last parting joke to me. I started walking down the road to my next destination, suitcase in one hand and my box of shit in the other.

Everything I owned now fit in my two tiny hands.

Aunt Julie

After losing home (or "base" as I liked to call it since it was more of just a safety net than a home to me), I spent even more time shuffling around, staying at different friends' houses, never staying anywhere more than two nights in a row.

I can't say I was sleeping at my friends' houses because by now I was doing so much speed that sleep was the thing that happened on accident while waiting for my next hit.

After a few months of this, I ended up falling at the feet of my uncle, who found me passed out in a booth at a gas station. He was coming in for some scratch-offs and just happened to see me slumped over. When I woke up, my immediate reaction was to cringe and try to run, his face being so similar to Mom's, only with a stale, blonde mustache. I finally came to my senses; he told me to get in his old Toyota. We were going to go get in a real bed so I could sleep this day off. I don't remember too much in between, seeing fields of cows and trees as I dozed in and out of sleep on the way to his place. I think it was the next day that I woke up. It felt like I had been asleep for a few years. My body was stiff and my muscles didn't want to move right, so I fell over a few times while trying to regain reality. My uncle, being an ex-addict himself, knew how I was feeling and had a sense of humor about it, making jokes at me as he made my breakfast.

His wife was at the kitchen table. A five foot, two inch lady with a permed mullet, pink metal-frame glasses and so much smokey eyeliner that it actually could have been smoke—especially with the few empty packs of cigarettes that lay by her USA eagle coffee mug, filled to the brim with instant Folgers.

"Well, howdy, Stranger!! You don't know me, but I'm your new aunt, Julie! How you feeling?" The thunderous twang that came out from tiny, stained teeth pierced my ears like two swords being jammed repeatedly in each canal. My uncle saw the interaction and knew by my tense face how I was feeling. He just began to laugh more.

"We decided you're gonna stay with us for a bit. You can share the room with the twins," he said as he plopped scrambled eggs and bacon on a plate in front of me.

It wasn't an ideal situation for me, as I wasn't used to being taken care of and my body had become accustomed to being on my own. For the first few weeks, it was not so bad...then reality started setting in. This place had rules; small ones, but rules nonetheless. They knew I was still using drugs, and tried to get me to stop. I began to see a different side of the once wide-eyed country lady that was now my aunt. I saw the same look that Mom had and it struck fear in me. There were nights she would just scream and cuss at me, telling me how worthless I was and that I needed to find another place to go. Uncle would have to come in and tell me she wasn't herself tonight and not to listen to her. I was getting antsy again, ready for my next move.

I think the last straw was when she found out that I had been smoking pot with her twin sons (had been almost the entire time I had been there). I was dealt a fair smack in the head and thrown out of the trailer. Shortly after, my grey suitcase came flying out. It opened and the few clothes I had were thrown across the yard. I said my fair choice of words back to her and began walking, not knowing where I was going, as I was ten miles out in the country.

After about an hour of walking, I saw headlights behind me and Uncle's familiar truck pulling up. He got me into the passenger seat and told me he had tried. He had my back, but he couldn't win this fight for me.

"I've contacted your mom and she said you could come stay with her for a bit. I wish things could be different, but I think you're aware of the limits you've crossed." And I think I was. Maybe I was just craving an escape, but instead what I got was a capture.

Back to the place I had hoped never to be again.

Linden

As I pulled down the oil-topped road with Uncle after a two-hour trek though town after nameless town, I began to realize that I was about to be even more isolated than before.

How i felt insIde.

The house we pulled up to was surprisingly nicer than I had expected. It was a double-wide trailer house set in the midst of a wooded area that hid the house until you passed the peak of the circle driveway. I knocked on the door; Mom and Uncle exchanged a few words and he was back off down the driveway. I got a weak, "Hi. There's some raviolis in the cabinet," as she walked back to her room to lie back in bed and watch her soaps.

Back to the apathetic parenting I was used to.

Being five miles from the heart of town, I knew I was going to have to make friends and make them quickly. My supply of drugs was running on empty. I knew one thing from shuffling around—a small town with nothing to do always meant you could find drugs easily. And that, I did.

Mom would drop me off at the gas station conveniently called *The Country Store*. Filled with fried chicken and day-old, deep-burned burritos, it was your typical backwoods station. (The other thing I had learned is that when people get stoned in small towns, this is the first place they go for snacks.) Within a few hours I had met up with the locals and established myself as being cool, a term that simply meant "not a narc".

Although I had connections now and could get high, I didn't really have any friends. I decided to go to the small Southern church with Mom one Sunday. Knowing my situation couldn't get any worse; I figured I might as well try. It was cheesy to say the least; almost like a bad car wreck, you couldn't take your eyes off it.

The pastor's son ended up approaching me, as he was the youth leader and it was probably part of his job. He was a few years older than me, maybe five or so, and had scraggly, comic book hair and gestures. I thought, out of everyone I had seen so far, he actually stood out. He didn't look like a white trash or a cowboy or a metal head—he looked normal. Well, normal to me…a kid with a shaved head save the two front bags that were down to my chin and always tucked behind my ears, and an arm full of bracelets and watches of all colors. This guy was normal and kind. The weird thing was, it didn't seem like he was faking his kindness. I thought, "Man, this guy is *good*. He must have been practicing the lines all day!"

I was intrigued, so I kept the conversation going to see how good his skill actually was, but he never faltered and always seemed genuine. I was determined to see the fakeness I had previously seen in everyone else who was a "Christian". It went on for weeks, then months, him picking me up and recording songs at his dad's church at all hours of the night. I didn't realize it, but this guy became my sponge, telling him details of my family life that I held deep in the secret places of my mind. Not that I was ready to be saved or anything, but it was nice to be exposed to a different kind of escape other than drugs. You could actually get weight off you by saying them aloud! Not all the weight, but at least enough to relieve some of the pressure. And I think the best part about it for me was that he never forced the Bible or religion on me—just was kinda there to be a voice of reason and an ear to listen.

Out of all the crazy things I did in that town and all the crazy things that happened to me, the little bit of light my friend showed me I know is what kept me going.

The Transition

After a few months of being in Linden, my parents got transferred back to Quitman. There was no way I was going to go back to that town with them, but it looked as if I didn't have a choice.

I got a call out of the blue from an old friend, asking if I wanted to jam with them in an old bank building that had been converted into a house.

teenage angst at its finest

I jumped at the opportunity, grabbed my guitar and hitched a ride to the studio apartment.

There were drums set up; my friend was already playing with his brother on the bass. I started setting up my gear. It consisted of my old, hand-me-down guitar and a tiny amp that I bought with money made from selling a bit of weed. What seemed like just a normal night of playing old Hendrix and Nirvana with my buddies turned out to be the Game Changer.

After we were done and the owner of the house and friend's brother had passed out on the couch from too many beers, my friend told me he was moving to Tyler in a few weeks. He wanted to know if I'd be interested in staying with him. I was excited, mostly because it meant I didn't have to stay with Mom. I was enticed by any place she wasn't.

The stipulation was that we would move up there, and I'd find a job and help out a little with the rent and food; he already had a job there. In my mind I was actually looking forward to not being a burden on someone and really, truly taking care of my own self. Game. Changer.

Moving Day just happened to fall on the same weekend Mom was moving back to Quitman, so I got a ride there with her, took my one suitcase and waited on the porch for Joey to show up with the moving truck and start my new adventure. The house we moved into was a red brick quad-plex, two downstairs apartments and two upstairs. We were on the bottom. There were nice wooden floors that opened up to a living room and a dining room, and a long narrow hallway leading to the bathroom and back bedroom that we shared. The house smelled of vintage grandma perfume, so we left a few windows and doors open to air it out as we moved everything in.

The air in Tyler felt different. It was new and a smidge of hope lay in its wind. At the moment, I didn't know it was hope, but I just knew I liked the scent.

music kept me balanced

CHAPTER FIVE
The House With The Hallway

The Caretaker

Living in Tyler was the beginning of a changing point in my life. Joey, my best friend, was more like my caretaker even though he was closer in age when compared to any other friends I had in the past. I put about ten percent effort into finding a job to help out with bills, but for the most part, I knew he would take care of me either way. It was a blind faith in something, maybe the first thing I ever really did put faith in.

The cool thing about Joey is that we never had an agenda—we just did what we wanted, whenever we wanted—aside from the hours he had to work to take care of us both. I remember countless hours just walking up and down the mall holding hands, pretending we were gay just to freak out the narrow-minded old people and rednecks that lived here.

One day they had Jacuzzis on display in the middle of the mall, all filled to the brim with water. Without even saying what we were doing, we casually got in, fully-clothed, and started lounging in the pool of steaming water. Of course security was on us in about five minutes. Joey always had an answer for authority figures.

"Son, I'm gonna have to ask you two to get out of there and vacate the mall."

"Son? That's strange—I thought my dad died from a car wreck because he was drunk driving. But you look good, Dad—nice to see you again!" was his snarky answer.

And I just lost it laughing when would come up with those snide remarks.

"Is there something funny, Son? I'm going to call the police and have you guys escorted somewhere far less nice."

With even less care I said, "Oh wow! You're not a cop, and you're MY dad too? Wow, then this is a way bigger deal than I thought it was."

And right as if Joey knew the perfect time to leave without getting in too much trouble, he signaled to me with a glance: we both just got out of the Jacuzzi and walked hand in hand back to his car. This kind of thing happened on a weekly basis, but somehow the worst we ever got was being told not to come back to the mall.

Which we ended up doing anyway.

Joey - the caretaker

my first guitar played til it broke in half

Emo Timmie

After being in Tyler for a few weeks, I still didn't have any local friends besides Joey. I was walking around the mall one day while he was at work and came across a group of people handing out flyers. I grabbed one from them—it was promoting a local punk rock show inside an abandoned storage shed not too far from our house. I thought it was as good a place as any to meet like-minded people...or at least someone from whom I could score some drugs.

When I got to the place, there were tons of people dressed all in black with slicked down, greasy black hair and dark, horn-rimmed glasses standing outside and about the storage shed. Most had their arms crossed; others were running into each other, knocking each other over, then picking them up. There was a guy with a silver beaded choker necklace screaming along to every word the band was screaming... or almost crying out really, since there was a lack of melody. The music was different than the grunge I was used to, or the hip-hop that had rhythm or the classic rock that had that vintage feeling. This was something new, like the guys playing didn't have a care in the world about how they conveyed their emotions. They were just releasing it all, exposing every hurt and detail of their life. And the message c onveyed well, as the crowd showed.

This guy looked at me and the first thing out of his mouth was, " What the fuck are you looking at?"

I kinda laughed at his bitterness and said, "Man, I'm just enjoying the experience."

"You're so emo."

"Maybe, dunno what that is. I'm Tim," and I held out my hand.

He was taken back by my response and just said, "I'm Austin. Follow me."

His bossiness was humorous to me, so I did follow him around as he proceeded to tell me who was "an asshole" and who was cool among everyone at the show. I was glad for his eagerness to talk since it was still not my best trait. With him I didn't need to talk; he would make up questions and answers for me. This began a friendship that would last a while as he introduced me to friends from whom I could get any drug I desired. He also had a car and could drive me to any place I wanted. I think my job was just to be there for him in return and listen to most of the things he said. After a few months he found out that I knew how to play the guitar.

"Hey, we're playing a show in Beaumont and our guitar player's mom won't let him go. You're our new guitar player. Get ready."

"Wait, wait...what? When?" I barely got the words out.

"We're leaving in thirty minutes."

"I can't learn an entire set worth of songs in thirty minutes! I can't even string my guitar and have it stay in tune in thirty minutes," I said as I pointed to the five strings on my guitar.

"It doesn't matter—it's emo. Just get your guitar and let's go."

As I was used to doing things on the fly and never really having a plan of action in anything, I agreed and put my beat-up Yamaha guitar with a missing string in the back of Austin's turquoise car. We were off.

He was right about it not mattering what it sounded like.

When we got there, the first band had already started; it was just a mixture of jumbled bar chords with someone's yelling voice over the top. I plugged into the same band's amp since I didn't bring one and our show began a few minutes later. I found delay and distortion pedals and just laid it on thick. A series of squelches and feedback came from the amp as Austin and his bandmates yelled and bashed through the set.

That night I got my first taste of stage fright. Seeing everyone watch me so intently, hanging on every move I made, I felt like I was being examined. Like I was being picked apart. I started losing my breath, panicking, and then without warning, my lunch came up to say hello. It was our third song and I was puking all over the stage, which was really just the floor of the storage shed. I threw down my guitar and ran off as it rang out the last feedback notes of the night.

I was mortified, feeling like a failure as I cleaned myself in a nearby bathroom. As I caught back on to reality, I heard the crowd screaming "PUNK ROCK!!" over and over. Cheers came as I walked back out. Everyone was high-fiving me, telling me that was the greatest thing they had ever seen. Maybe I was just stoned, but these people seemed to be the most easily pleased people on the planet. I didn't care—I suppose my disappointment turned into pride.

Maybe I had something going with this music thing.

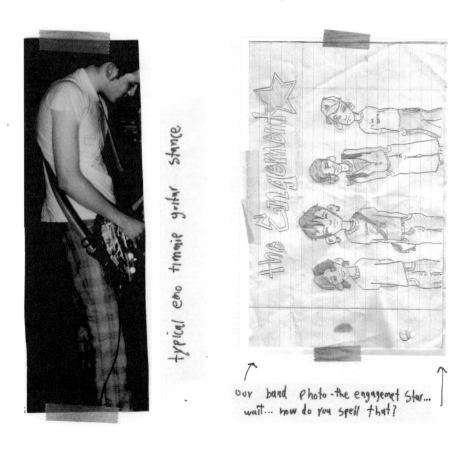

typical emo timmie guitar stance

our band photo -the engagemet star... wait... how do you spell that?

A New Family

After I met Austin, things started seeming pretty normal, my daily life and the friends I was making outside of just Joey.

I even started having contact with Mom again. She would come to Tyler ever so often and visit me. When she visited, she would give me scratch-off lotto tickets that she won—$5 here, $20 there. I would save them up, then cash them in and give the money to Joey to show an effort. I think he appreciated it somewhat, but deep down he wanted me to pull more weight than I was at the time.

The last time Mom came to see me, we ended up getting in an argument due to her thinking that I took some drugs out of the car as we were riding around. I could tell she was a little off by the way she was acting, so I just told her to drop me off and I would walk the rest of the way home. I didn't hear from her for a few days after that until I got a call from Stepdad telling me that Mom went off the rocker again. In our house that term was just known as: *Mom tried to kill herself.*

Every time she did this, I struggled with thinking it was my fault whether I had anything to do with it or not. Mostly from the fact that she would tell me, "You boys drive me to this point. You know that, don't you?" So I couldn't help but have a little guilt about the fight we had just had and the mean things we had said to each other in anger. Austin came over about an hour after I got the phone call, and even though he seemed harsh and impenetrable on the outside, he was pretty intuitive about life in general...and toward me specifically. He just said two words.

"What's wrong?"

I lost it, my eyes filled with tears of guilt and hate as I struggled to get the indecipherable words out.

"Get in the car. I know where we need to go."

We drove for about seven minutes until we reached the outskirts of town and pulled up a long circle driveway to an older house surrounded by woods. As I got out I saw a mixture of little, blonde-headed beautiful people, one after another, gradually getting older and older. Austin asked if "Mom" was here. They pointed to the back bedroom.

I looked into the eyes of Mama DuPree; it was the first time I had seen that kind of emotion portrayed through anyone. It felt as if she was warming me with blankets of hope, just using the emotion pouring from her eyes. When she heard my situation, she began to speak. I felt as if I could have curled up and slept for days at her feet. The calm gentle vibrations flew from her mouth with ease. It was something so new and inviting to me, the only response I could give was to cry more. It was like her words were filling up the darkness that had been dwelling inside of me all those years and it was being forced out in the form of tears, making my entire body weak. I crumbled as the dad, Boyd, caught me and spoke the same gentle words into me.

That day lit a spark in me. No matter how many more bad things I would do in my life and wrong decisions I would make; I knew I had a chance of hope. Each Sunday after that, either they or a friend would come by my house and take me to their church. Every Friday when that church became a venue for bands to play, they had someone pick me up and make sure I was in a safe place, even if it was just for a few hours. They took me in anytime I thought Joey was getting frustrated with me being there, mooching off him. Some weeks I would spend four or five days at a time sleeping on their floor. Definitely one of the reasons I'm still here today to tell this story lies in the soft words and comfort of their love.

a new family

Fredophile

I think maybe I was a super attractive kid. Or maybe I looked vulnerable or maybe there are just more creepy people in a bigger town than I was used to. Plus the naiveté of my mind was still in full bloom.

As I walked to see my new family, the DuPrees, I stopped at a gas station to pick up a Gatorade and some gum. When I walked out, there was a tall bulky man that looked like he had been working out nonstop for the past week. Sweat dripping from his forehead, he shot me a toothy, half-curled smile. Non-thinking, I smiled back and started to walk on to my destination, but before I could reach the curb, he stopped me.

"Hey, can I give you a ride or somethin'?"

"Nah, I'm fine. Just going down the road anyways, " I said, barely glancing up at him.

"Naaahhh, get in. Iss too hot fo you be walkin'. Imma good guy—get in!" he said with that toothy grin.

I got into his old pickup that smelled of grease and ashes and we started riding away from the direction I had intended on going, but I figured he knew a back way or something.

"I'm Fred; I'm yo new friend. You live 'round here?"

"I'm kinda in and out of places. I think you might have missed my turn back there," I said with hesitation.

"Aaahh, thas ok. I need to go pick sumthin' up real quick—only take a second. That cool?"

I just nodded, getting a tight feeling in my stomach that I tried to shake. A fear was creeping in on me, but my pride wouldn't let it show. I had been in way stickier situations than this.

A few minutes passed, getting further and further away from where I had intended on going. Finally, we pulled up to a duplex on the south side of the city. I recognized where I was after seeing the Walmart and Target.

"Come on in, this'll take a minute or two." He motioned me in the door. "Have a seat; I'll make you a drink. You like tea?"

"Well, I still have my Gatorade. I'm fine."

I think he chose not to hear that last sentence as he came back with something he called his "Long Island Iced Tea." Must be some kind of special recipe because when I took that first drink, I thought my heart was going to explode. It was the most sour tea I had ever tasted—and I think he could tell. He kinda laughed when he saw my face at the taste of the sour concoction. A few minutes later he was fumbling through some VHS tapes and put in a movie called *The Specialist*, some spy action movie that I wasn't really interested in. I was still trying to hold my fear down and prove that I was an adult and could handle my own, so I just pretended to be engaged.

As I sat there, he came back from the kitchen with some steak fingers he had cooked up in his oven. They were on a plate with ketchup—my true weakness, food. I didn't care what this stuff was poisoned with, it couldn't be any worse than the tea, so I gladly ate up and waited for him to get through doing whatever he needed to do so I could get on with my day. I sat and waited in silence through at least an hour and a half of the movie, but right when it was getting to the good part and I actually cared what happened to the characters, he gets up and takes out the cassette! Then he puts in an unmarked tape and all of a sudden, two naked girls and a greasy, old mustached man were going at it like crazy on the screen. He must have watched this previously because he started telling me what was about to happen as if it were a play-by-play game analysis.

"And now this new guy's gonna come in and..."

"You know you can tell that's real…"

"Would you ever do that to another guy?" was his last question before I stopped him.

"Hell no!! That's sooo nasty! I'm not like that! I think you might have the wrong idea—it's time for me to go." This took him off guard.

"Damn, you don't have to be like that, I was just asking. It's just porn—everybody has these thoughts. Don't freak out!"

"I don't have these thoughts," I said as I got up and walked to the door.

"At least let me give you a ride back."

I slammed the door before he had a chance to finish his sentence and started to run to Walmart. I stayed there all-day, walking around and lounging in the outdoor area on the swings until Joey got off work. He called and I had him pick me up.

I saw Fred a few more times around the city, but maybe his knowledge that I could call the police on him (after all I was still a kid!) or that I wouldn't give in to the things he wanted kept him from pursuing me.

I still never finished that first movie though.

First Job

Finally all my feeble attempts to get a job paid off. I found a place that didn't care that I was fifteen and didn't have a high school education—Jack In The Box. I went in with high hopes, my first day consisting of watching funny old training videos in the back. I could do this—how hard would it be to make hamburgers and french-fries? I knew how to use a microwave. A fryer and grill couldn't be much different, right?

Each day there was a new challenge thrown into the mix: how to use the soda machine, how to work the bread toaster, and on and on. The week went on and without realizing it; the job was stressing me out. The sounds of seven different buzzers going off at once, plus the heat and grease from the grill popping up on my hands—my anxiety would soon get the best of me.

I had to work a morning/lunch shift so I stayed up all night to be sure not to oversleep for the big day ahead of me. I got to work and already a line of people were stacked in the main lobby, plus carloads wanting food in the drive thru. Everyone had a look as if they were about to face the death of a loved one. Hungry, desolate-faced and the same attitudes to go along with it.

I was making eight burgers at a time and taking orders with my earpiece all in the same breath. Then the beeping that had been going on forever in the midst of the chaos came to my attention because of the smell. I was burning buns. One of the managers started yelling and taking the buns out frantically. As he walked by, I caught his eyes on the fryer of deep dark curly fries that had also been sitting far too long. When I came to, I had almost given the meat patties the same fate, and someone in my ear was now yelling.

"Hello?? Are you there?? Did you get my order?!"

My forehead was sweating and my heart felt like one hundred tiny men were beating it to an erratic rhythm. My breaths couldn't come fast enough and I felt there might not be another, so I started trying to take them in even faster. Everything had built up so high, the tension became like the friction of rocks being dragged and forced against a chalkboard, and I finally exploded.

"FUUUUUUUUCKKK YOUUUUUUUUU!!!!!!"

Over the intercom. To the patrons outside. To my co-workers, patrons and boss inside. There wasn't another sound for five seconds as everyone just stared at me. Tears of anger (or insanity) were flowing down my face, red and sweaty.

I finished making the two hamburgers I had been working on before the explosion, meticulously adding every ingredient. I took them and the over-cooked fries and put them in a brown paper sack, then walked over and grabbed the biggest cup we had. Filling it to the brim with ice and strawberry soda, throwing my headset back toward the grill as I walked out.

Halfway home I realized the degree of what had just happened and had to sit down. I stayed in the park for a good two hours, eating my last Jack In The Box meal and letting relief come to me.

The sounds gone.

The people gone.

The smell gone.

It looked like the work world just wasn't for me. The next morning I awoke to a phone call at six am.

my best attempt at a smile

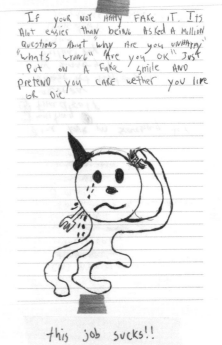

If your not HAPPY FAKE iT. Its Alot easier than being Asked A Million Questions About "why Are you uNHAPPY" "whats wrong" "Are you OK" Just Put on A Fake smile AND pretend you CARE wether you live or Die

this job sucks!!

"Uummm, Tim, where are you at?"

"What do you mean, where am I at? You called me. I'm at my house, obviously asleep. Who is this?" I mumbled.

"This is your boss, and if you don't come in, I'm going to have to terminate you."

Confused, I didn't know how to respond. "Umm, were you not at the same place I was yesterday?"

"Well, does that mean you're not coming in?"

"NO!! BYE." Click.

That ended my job career for this chapter of my life.

Tattoo Birthday

Of all the people I met, one happened to be a tattoo artist. Always being attracted to the idea and to people who had tattoos, I asked if she would give me one. She asked if I knew what I wanted—I really had no clue. She told me to think about it for a few weeks, draw something whenever I wanted it and just try it out for a bit, to see if I liked it enough to get it permanently.

I took her advice, but I'm no artist. I let Austin attempt a few things, but after he took it as a joke and drew penises and choice words all over me, I went back to more basic things. There was a girl with whom I was really good friends and she asked if I had ever considered a star.

"It can represent so many different things. I think for you, there is Someone up above looking down on you and keeping you safe. Your star above."

The way she said it, with such authority in her voice, stuck with me for a long time. I drew a star on my right hand in the tiny space of skin between my thumb and first finger. But with me treating life as a joke all the time, I couldn't just have some serious, deeply meaningful tattoo. I needed something that people expected of me—something people would think was funny and I would too. On the other hand I proceeded to draw two eyes on the side of my first finger and a mouth on the edge of my thumb so I could make a funny face, talk to people and generally be a goon with my hand.

As my fifteenth birthday grew closer, I had been trying out my permanent marker face and star on people. Most everyone encouraged me to get the face, but when I got to the tattoo shop, I heard a man say, "I'm looking out for you."

I looked up, expecting to see someone talking to me, but it was just a man outside the shop on his phone. Even after having my mind set, that triggered something in me that was confirmed by my tattoo artist friend.

"NO. I'm not drawing a dumb face on you. You'll regret it in the future. Trust me."

I laughed and shook my head, agreeing with her. As she prepared my hand, my body started to tense up; I was getting nervous. The first prick just made me laugh because I had never felt a pain quite like it and my body didn't know any other way to react. I felt life leaving my body.

"OH MY GOD, are you going to pass out?" she yelled.

"NO. Keep going," I said in unsure breaths of laughter as she handed me a couple of Jolly Ranchers to suck on. Said the sugar would help me.

In a matter of about five minutes, my permanent reminder of that day was done, and I had a feeling of pride and accomplishment. I went through a painful experience and had something to show for it, a reward that I had never experienced from previous pains.

To this day, I still think the face tat would have been funny. Maybe next time.

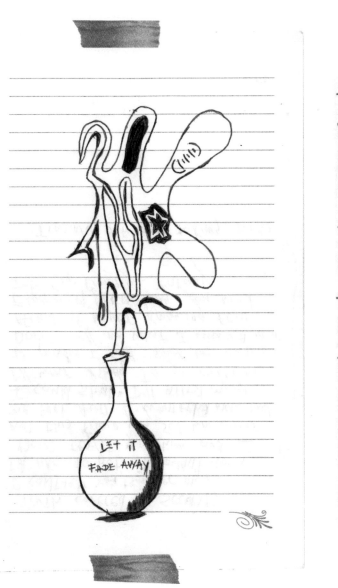

on acid shapes and objects took the form of water.
hence most of my druggy art follows that same pattern.

Let it
FADE AWAY

Mallrats

After having tons of friends over the years (some that are just a faint memory or idea of a friend), obviously there were friends that I liked more than "just friends." But due to my shyness, their lack of interest or one girl having a huge 6'1" cross-dressing husband that didn't approve of our relationship (I won't get into that one), it never really worked out. There was one girl in particular that I had had a crush on since my second year in seventh grade, Kelli.

Although she was from the same small town as me and grew up with all the same backwoods people, she was different. That's probably the main thing that attracted me to her. She wore all the same dirty bracelets and had the same habit of changing her hair, dying it different colors every week. She just wasn't like everyone else in our small town.

She ended up moving to Tyler as well and I made the mistake of introducing her to my friend Austin. I've never known myself to be jealous of anything, but I became that way as soon as they met. Envious that this kid who hated everything and had so much negative energy had such an influence over the girl I thought I might actually have a chance with. I soon let that go, trying to let them be happy. After awhile, I saw they were more alike than I had thought.

Although Austin was nice to me, he wasn't the easiest person for other people to get along with. He made enemies everywhere we went and almost caused a few fights because of his temper about life. Needless to say, he wasn't the best boyfriend to Kel either. I never really talked to him about her, but I figured as much by the conversations I would overhear him having while he was at the house.

We were out in the mall just a few days after he had one of these not-so-pleasant conversations with Kel, looking for a new earring he could use for a nose piercing he had recently gotten. In the middle of the mall was a store called *Afterthoughts*, filled to the brim with things you might see on a twelve year old rich girl trying to impress all her middle school friends. Feather boas, sunglasses, nail polish and cheap jewelry were oozing out of the open walls of the store. For me this store was magic, but I couldn't see Dark Everything Austin finding anything in it.

He went to a corner where one of the workers was stocking new necklaces and started talking like he knew her. This wasn't strange for Austin; he seemed to know everyone. I was drawn to the front counter where there were piles of nail polish in all colors. One thing I loved more than anything was bright, vibrant colors. I think my outfit spoke for itself. I had on tan Dickies with bright red Converse that were colored on and marked up with polish, as well as cross-stitched pink shirt reading "Grandma's my name, spoilin's my game" and a matching pink cardigan. My hair was freshly shaven in the back with two front pieces hanging down past my chin and tucked behind each ear, bright pink on one side and dark purple on the other. My nails already had black paint chipping away on them, but I was always in the market for more.

In my own world, I finally looked up and came back to reality when I saw the eyes I would never forget. A mixture of hazelish green and brown, touched with diamonds. I couldn't help but stare as if she was purposely putting me into a trance. The expression on her face completely contrasted the way her eyes were speaking to me and I was jolted back. She wore an expression as if I had spilled paint all over her and completely ruined her day. Then the words came out of her mouth.

"What, are you some kind of cross-dresser or something?"

It cut deep and I didn't know any other way to answer but with sincere honesty. These words came fumbling out of my own mouth.

"No...I just like pretty things."

At that, the tension and angst she had toward me began to dissipate and those kind eyes started to match the new expression she had. At the same moment, I recognized the girl Austin was talking to—it was Kelli's older sister. She had seen the interaction between Diamond Eyes and me and rushed over.

"NO, NOT HIM! That's Timmie. We like Timmie. That guy over there is Austin—he's the one being a jerk to Kelli."

I immediately saw the girl's face start to turn a light shade of pink. To diffuse the situation, I said "Hey, now you match my shirt!" and gave a kind of laugh. I knew comedy always made awkward things better—or at least funnier.

She stuck out her tiny little hand and said, "Hi, I'm DeAnda. Want to come to our house and play?"

I laughed and greeted her kindness with a half smile, too embarrassed to giver her a full one. She was a perfect beauty, unlike any friend I had ever had before. I'm not saying I didn't think my other friends were beautiful, but she was a different kind. She was someone to whom nothing bad had ever happened, someone that wasn't jaded by life and was still soft.

I could tell in her eyes that she meant everything she wasn't telling me with her mouth—that there would be more to this meeting than either of us knew.

always doodling to keep my mind busy.

pretty much the exact outfit from this story

Y2K

Y2K. It was the dreaded transition from 1999 to 2000 and the computers were going crash and kill us all—yay!

I think it was more than appropriate to throw a huge party and celebrate.

My friends and I were discussing it, some actually believing the hype a lot; others thought that if the world was going to end on Y2K night then it would ruin our party. Of course the obvious answer was to have it three nights before New Year's Day. So that was that.

I remember being in a strange place kind of close to the lake. You could see a dock and people with beer bottles and acoustic guitars sitting on it. There were piles of cars in the yard and an assortment of people. Some looked as if they were barely in high school, where some looked like they had been out of it for twenty or more years. I sat down with someone I knew from going to the local punk rock shows and started smoking a joint with him.

"It's laced with formaldehyde, man," he mumbled out while still taking in a hit of smoke.

I vaguely remembered it having to do with a funeral home and said, "Like the stuff they put on dead people?"

"I think, man. Waking the dead!!" He laughed and I did too.

I only smoked a little of that. The smell of the smoke was so strong and unpleasant that I had to walk off. A few minutes later I found some more kids smoking and started tokin' up with them. This one was laced with Angel Dust. I could tell because it had a different sour tinge to the smoke as well.

"Doesn't anyone smoke regular old pot anymore?" I complained jokingly.

"Aaahhh, a purist! What, man, you don't like hallucinations with your high? Over there in the corner is probably more your flavor—that's where all the hippies are." He kinda laughed and went back to what he was doing.

As I made my way over to the tie-dyed mess in the corner, I knew I was in the right spot. A girl with a flower wreath she had made out of the weeds and brush surrounding the house handed me two tiny squares of paper that had a picture of Felix the Cat juggling something. The pieces were so tiny I took them up closer to my eye to see what I couldn't from afar. The silence was interrupted by the girl.

"It's planets. Felix. He's juggling the planets. Put them in your mouth. You'll understand...he juggles all of us." I thought she was joking and I laughed as I put them in my mouth, letting the paper dissolve and numb my tongue. Within half an hour it started to kick in, but I wasn't sure in which order, as I had been drinking mushroom-infused tea and smoking some of the "natural hippy weed" while I waited for Felix to start juggling me. Plus, there was also the chemically enhanced mess I had smoked previously.

The sun began to dance as she fell into the water. The water opened up and swallowed the sun whole, spitting out stars back into the sky one by one, as if they were watermelon seeds.

It was almost like the lake was playing a game—the stars began to make patterns like a dot-to-dot book and I slowly let my mind wander, drawing people and animals in the sky from star to star. With each person and thing I drew, the sky would become more crowded as everything was dancing to the music. Once it would get too full, I'd just take my hand and swipe it across the sky and all the lines I had drawn would fall back into the lake. Then the game would start all over. I remember lying down and almost giving in to the heaviness of sleep taking me over. It must have been hours that I was staring, playing this game, because I saw the sun emerging from her nest again.

Right at the brink of sleep, I was handed a small straw made from a pen and told to sniff in the goodness. I did, as hard as I could, and the burning that trickled from my nose all the way behind my eyes and down my throat was enough to jolt me wide open. I was running. I was happy and I felt free. The world was ending in one day and this was the best way to go out.

I repeated everything from the previous day, only even more weed and even more acid and even more speed until I got to the point where it felt like the only thing still working was my determination to stay awake. People were leaving or passing out one by one. Then the cops came and people scattered. I saw the guy I came with leaving, so in my zombie state of mind, I quickly got in his car.

I got back home sober enough to keep my cool in front of Joey when he got home, but high enough to feel horrible. It was nighttime and I washed myself up a bit before Joey got home at eleven on New Year's Eve. He asked how I wanted to celebrate Y2K, not knowing I had been out doing just that for the last few days.

I just said, "Flush it," so we went into the bathroom and stood there counting down the seconds. "5, 4, 3, 2, 1" hand in hand we both flushed the toilet—something random like we always did, but it would come to have more meaning than I even knew.

As he was exhausted from work and I was exhausted from the last couple of days, we both went to bed. As I lay there feeling like death, letting sleep take my body home, I thought about how I wished I was in that toilet flushing away, realizing that not even drugs were making me happy. I didn't get to contemplate this long as I was asleep before I could have a chance to finish my train of thought.

I woke up periodically in a cold sweat over the next few days, puking from hour to hour. In between dreams and nightmares and being sick, I would see those kind hazel eyes, wishing I had someone to watch over me that had that much care and compassion. I thought if I ever wake up, I'm going to take her up on that offer to come over and play. From that second on, I knew drugs and I were through. I had flushed them from my mind.

Forever Begins Now

Always going in circles

A New Best Friend

About a week or two had passed and somehow the computers didn't kill us all like everyone thought they would, so me and Joey were back to our daily ritual of mall walking and driving around listening to music without saying a word. It was pretty much the same; only without drugs I felt everything. I could feel the tremors in my stomach rumbling when I got hungry, and feel the pain that followed if I didn't do anything about it. I felt the sadness of past thoughts weighing on me like lead in water. I could feel my body aching and wanting me to have drugs again. I didn't like this new feeling, but knew I couldn't go back to the old feeling now.

As we were in the mall, we stopped by that same kids' jewelry store again. The relief of my anticipation was settled—the beautiful diamond-eyed girl was working, or finishing work, I should say—counting bills and putting them in a zipper envelope. She lit up when she saw me and said, "Timmie!" as if we had been best friends all of our lives. This was quite a change from the first interaction we had and I welcomed it.

"Are you coming to our party tonight?" Before I had a chance to answer, she spoke up for me. "Of course you are; you can ride with me. Come on, I have to make a deposit."

With that I was being whisked away in the backseat of a car with Dee and Kel's sister. It was as if instantly we knew what to say and in minutes we were all laughing and joking about absolutely nothing at all. This was just the beginning of a special bond that would change my whole perspective on life.

As quickly as we got to the house, there were already people falling in the door—mostly college-age guys, a few people I recognized from back in my old town and a few locals I had seen here and there. There was alcohol lined up in the kitchen of the upstairs apartment where Dee and her friend lived. I remember hearing her say, "I'm not drinking tonight; I had way too much at New Year's." This was a great relief to me, seeing how I had never liked alcohol to begin with...and there would also be at least one like-minded person to talk to.

I saw Kelli as I passed the corner into the living room; she was well on her way already. My heart didn't skip the same beat anymore at the sight of her face and the sound of her name being spoken. It was confusing to say the least, but I let it pass. I'm guessing that Dee and her roommate knew about my crush on Kelli because they kept hinting things about her all night like, "You know she and Austin are not together right now, right?" and "You know, you and Kel would make a cute couple." Normally this kind of talk would have me so excited that it would drown out all other thoughts, but it wasn't doing it for me. I felt like I should still try and get closer to her, but the intrigue was gone now.

By the end of the night, I had lost sight of her. People were starting to fall asleep on floors and couches and staircases. Dee came up to me and said, "Now's your chance—Kelli is in that room alone. Perfect time to talk to her!" I felt encouraged that she even thought I would be a good match for any girl, so I built up my courage and walked in the room.

The smell took me back. It was like someone had left Koolaid and a bag of oranges in a box of kitty litter for weeks and forgot about it. I called out to Kel and just heard a faint "Huuuhhh...whaaaat?" from the corner. I slowly walked out a few seconds after I went in and Dee asked what happened.

"Ummm, Kel is on the floor with puke all over her."

Dee's reaction was an almost laugh and a sympathy, "Awwww." I didn't know if that was for me or her, but she said, "Come on, we can sleep here in the hallway. You put your head that way and I'll put mine like this. That way we can see if each other is awake."

Neither one of us slept that night. We stayed up talking, telling secrets to each other or sometimes just laughing. She told me of her boyfriend in college and how she

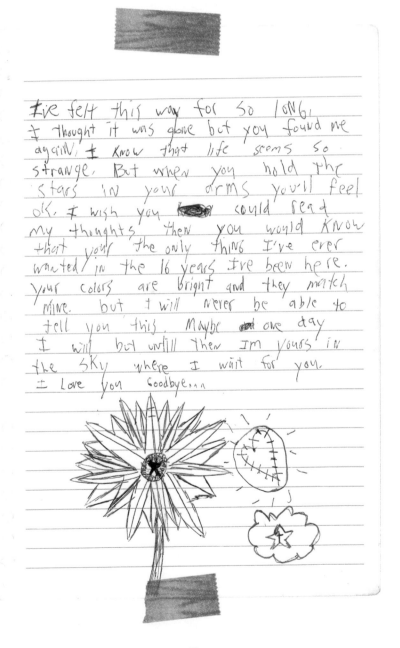

I've felt this way for so long, I thought it was gone but you found me again, I know that life seems so strange. But when you hold the stars in your arms you'll feel ok. I wish you could read my thoughts then you would know that your the only thing I've ever wanted in the 16 years I've been here. your colors are bright and they match mine. but I will never be able to tell you this. Maybe one day I will but untill then Im yours in the sky where I wait for you. I love you Goodbye...

just recently decided to stop drinking. She told me stories of her childhood; I only let little bits of mine slip out, each time with an even bigger reaction than the last. It was the beginning of tons of nights like this.

In the next few weeks she kept getting more bits of my story, and sometimes in the middle of me telling something, I would suddenly just get up and start running out the door, telling her I'd be right back. I had been super sick, my body readjusting to not having drugs, so I would throw up once or twice a day at sporadic times. I was too embarrassed to tell her what I was doing. I figured she would chalk it up to me just being a weird boy. I never made it more than halfway down the street before I threw up and felt good enough to come back. After a week or two of this behavior, she finally got it out of me and to my surprise, didn't pass any judgment whatsoever. It was nice; for the first time in my life, I felt I had a safety—someone I didn't have to worry about what I told. A new best friend.

I knew I didn't have any chance of ruining this either, since she had a college boyfriend and I never even graduated high school. I didn't even *make* it to high school. I tried to trick myself out of having feelings for her, but I decided against doing that. I would just keep it a secret. No one has to know everything...right?

Valentine's Day

Valentine's Day. A day celebrated and advertised on TV and in stores with mushy sayings and cheesy acts of kindness.

A day I never ever celebrated.

It was more of a day that I looked at as a milestone; I had almost made it through another year since my birthday was February 15th. It was how I always remembered I was turning another year older, although I was never sure what age "older" was.

This particular year I was actually with someone on Valentine's Day, not in the way my heart desired, but at least in the same room *with* a girl. Her boyfriend was still away at college, hours from here, and all day she waited for flowers or a phone call, but nothing yet. I kept her mind off of the Valentine's idea as best I could—the only way I knew how—by just being myself and acting goofy, making her laugh all day.

Finally, at about eight o'clock the call she had been waiting on was happening, so I gave her a little bit of privacy as she began to talk in the other room. A few minutes later, I heard a loud, "What?! Are you kidding me? ON THE WEED??? He doesn't even do that anymore. You're ridiculous!"

After that it got really quiet. A few minutes later, she came out of the bedroom and back to where I waited. Her eyes were glistening with water, and she wore a con-fused look on her face like she had misplaced something. I asked if she was okay. She sat down on the couch as if her legs were giving out, so close beside me that her legs were touching mine. My heart began to race.

"He dumped me because he thought I was "on the weed" with you," she trickled out between sobs. I didn't mean to, but at the phrase "on the weed," I just started laughing.

"'On the weed'? Hahaha…who in the world were you dating?"

At that, she let out a relief of laughter between the tears and I knew she approved of my reaction. I felt her body losing the control to be upright on its own, so I grabbed her head and positioned her on the couch so I could be her support and pillow. I didn't really say much for the next hour, but let her get emotions out through tears and little remarks here and there as I gently stroked her soft hair back behind her ears. I think it was the first time I realized how delicate she actually was, other than the first time she shook my hand; her hair was so smooth it felt like my hands were melting as I ran my fingers through it.

That night I felt a change in the air between us. I wasn't sure if she felt it too, but I wasn't going to ask and ruin the feeling. I just accepted it and let it bring us closer together.

Within the next few days, Dee was completely back to her old fun self, and we were having even more fun that we had before, sharing even more of each others' pasts and secrets. She met Mom for the first time. Within the first five minutes, Mom had already told a few sexual jokes and made Ninja Turtle action figures do inappropriate things while laughing about it. Dee just laughed awkwardly as I said, "Yup, that's my mom..."

I didn't know how to be embarrassed really, and with Dee, I didn't have to. She would accept all the crazy facts about my life, most of which I never even knew were crazy until I started telling her. I remember her saying, "Ummm, that's not normal... things like this are not supposed to happen." I would proceed by apologizing and she would always have a rebuttal, telling me it wasn't my fault. No one had made me feel as special and as important as her. Ever. My feelings were growing and growing, as well as the urge to reveal these things to her. I knew I couldn't though—there was no way I could ruin this relationship like I had so many others in my life.

By now we were spending pretty much every second she had free together. I would be waiting at her doorstep the second she got home and we would usually stay up all night. Finally, two or three hours before she had to be at work the next day, we would let each other sleep. She had started kissing my forehead every night where I slept on the couch before she went to her bedroom down the hall. So many nights I wished she would miss my forehead and hit my lips!

After about a month of this had gone on, one night we shared some of our hardest secrets with each other and she lay down on the tiny couch built for only one. She was pressed up against me, snuggling and showing her love by surrounding me in her warmth. Her hug only lasted about a minute, but it felt like days had gone on in my mind. I didn't want it to end. This time she kissed my forehead...then she kissed it again. Then my right cheek. My left. My body flooded with so many emotions and thoughts that I couldn't control myself anymore. I leaned to the right as she was coming to kiss my other cheek and planted my lips against hers, grabbing the back of her head to keep balance so I wouldn't ruin the moment by falling over in excitement. The kiss seemed to last even longer than the hug and after it was over, a fear hit my entire body.

What had I done? Did I ruin everything? Was I about to be slapped?

The awestruck look in her eyes told it all. When she was getting up to go to bed, she told me she loved me as she had always done, but this time there was a totally different tone in her voice, a tone deeper and more sincere than any words I had ever heard. Those words crushed and surrounded me like a warm glove, as if they had so much weight to keep me on the couch forever. Our eyes were glued to each other's souls as I told her I loved her, too. She gave me the softest peck right on the center of my upper lip and walked away to her bed.

I don't remember ever falling asleep that night as I just lay there with the biggest smile I could muster. I didn't want to fall asleep because I was afraid I would wake up and it all would have been a dream.

The next day things did change, but only for the better. We began walking together, holding hands and kissing more, but not in front of anyone yet. It was a fun little secret we got to share. It was thrilling, knowing this beautiful girl and me, the rejected boy, were falling for each other, falling harder every day.

Finally, after a couple of weeks of almost showing affection in public, we decided to just freak everyone out. Someone made a joke about how funny it would be if we just started making out. I looked into Dee's eyes and knew it was the time. Right in the same place where we met in the mall, in front of a group of our friends and any mall spectators that happened to be looking, I laid a huge kiss on her. Over-dramatically of course, since that's the only way we both did things. We fell to the floor kissing as I heard laughs and gasps from everyone. It was a buildup of emotions that led to an explosion...finally our secret was out! We could be that annoying couple who loved each other and had to be in every inch of each other's space at all times. And I loved it.

I was happy. I was free. I felt I had a purpose and I felt special.

The days were beginning to change.

Backstreet Birthday

Backstreet's back, alright.

That's right—one of my favorite things about Dee was her Backstreet Boys obsession. She and her roommate were far too old to have such a crush, but I think that's what made it cute and funny to me. They had all the *Tiger Beat* magazines and VHS tapes of live concerts lying around their house. I would get informed who was who and what their favorite activities/food/color was. I knew it was ridiculous, and they knew it too, but it was a fun thing we did.

For Dee's birthday they had gotten two Backstreet Boys tickets for Dallas and asked if my friend Joshie and I wanted to go with them. They didn't have tickets for us, but knew we could find something to do during the concert if we were together, being who we were with our quirky personalities. Of course I agreed; it just meant I got to spend more time with Dee, which I was always down for. We had a big video camera that we used to document the whole weekend with...which ended up being more of an advantage than we initially thought.

The first night (since it was a two night concert and the girls only had tickets for the second night) we just went to the parking lot and they filmed me yelling at all the crazy fans. And eventually yelling at Brian, one of the Backstreet Boys. I was yelling "Brian looks like a monkey, Brian looks like a monkey!" to which he just looked up at me, confused. The part that was the most fun was just making Dee laugh and seeing joy in her eyes. By now, I would do anything for that girl.

The next night Josh and I dropped the girls at the door of the concert, giving high fives and hugs. We had our huge, shoulder-crushing video camera and were on our way. We found every TV station that was doing a story and stood by them, acting a fool, and ended up being on every channel in the DFW area. The same thing happened with all the radio stations.

A few hours in, we were just videoing and interviewing any random stranger we could find when a bouncer approached us. We thought our days of mayhem were over, but instead he asked, "Are you coming in or not?"

We pretended we knew exactly what to do and started walking into the backstage area when we were stopped again. "So close!" we thought—but then came another surprise.

"You're gonna need these first." The same bouncer grabbed our hands and attached an orange paper bracelet on each of our wrists. It read "All Access Backstage Party." Joshie and I were trying everything we could to hold in our laughter as we walked into a backstage area of Reunion Arena.

"Am I even old enough to drink?" I said to Josh.

"You? Hahaha—*I'm* not even old enough to drink." He laughed out loud as we were in what looked like a night club, neon lights and drinks everywhere. There was a bar area lit up by beer signs and bartenders making things I had never even heard of before. We could hear the concert going on as if it were right on the other side of the wall lined with high bar stools and tiny tables. The smoke was so bad that I started to not be able to breath right.

"Let's get out of here. This is lame," I said.

Some drunk girl was asking Josh if we were from MTV; he just kept a straight face and told her of course we were. I think we would have gotten to meet the Backstreet Boys if we had stayed in there, but a tiny bit of me was jealous of them. Even though Dee made me feel special, I knew I didn't have what they had, so I didn't want to have that competition.

We left as the concert was ending and walked around to the door the girls had entered. They looked at our orange bracelets. "Of course you two did. Of course."

It turned out that the Boys were not going to the VIP area anyway, as we saw them heading toward their tour bus. Dee was wearing angel wings the entire night and as she saw them walk out, she ripped them off, throwing them as hard as she could over the fence and toward the forty-foot drop off down to the Boys and their bus. They got stuck at the very top of the fence, so I jumped up and slapped them as hard as I could. They began to slowly drift down toward the walking, smiling Boys.

As Kevin, the black-haired Backstreet Boy saw them, he sat and stared, slowly waiting for the wings to come down. Then he grabbed them and pretended to fly away to the bus to a series of screams. "KEVINNN!!!"

As silly as it was, I felt a sense of accomplishment as I saw how happy it made Dee. She looked at me, gave me a huge hug and a kiss right there in front of everyone. Maybe I did have something that a Backstreet Boy didn't have.

I had my diamond-eyed girl.

Tylenot

Dee's mom was back in Quitman, so we went down there for a visit and for her to introduce me to her mom. She didn't think it would go over well if she told her that we were a thing, so I told her she didn't have to; we met as friends. She was taken back by me; I could see it in her eyes. She had the same care in them as Dee, but there was a hesitation that blocked her from fully understanding who I was...and me from fully understanding her. A mental brick wall, so to speak. It was ok since I was used to most people not fully relating. She was sweet enough anyway. I got to see some of the characteristics that Dee had and understand where they came from a little bit more.

Our visit only lasted a little bit over an hour, then we decided to go to Mom's house. We pulled up one of the main roads in Quitman to her driveway, where the stench of rabbit manure was already putrid our noses before we even opened the door. There were still about one hundred rabbits Stepdad kept in the backyard for shows and for eating when they got too big.

As we walked in the house, the smell didn't get any better. There was dog crap in every corner of the room...under tables...beside couches and chairs. Half empty bowls of what used to be food laid about, as well as banana peels and brown apple cores, dried up and growing who knows what on them. There on the couch sat Mom, lopped down watching soaps on an old boxy TV sitting on top of an even older console TV that didn't work. There was no need to ask why she didn't throw the old TV away since she never threw away anything, apparently not even trash. Plus the old TV was serving a purpose—if it wasn't there to hold the slightly newer one, Mom might get a crick in her neck from looking down too much.

The rest of the house was trashed even worse; only one room was even slightly clean—my brother's old bedroom. There were about a hundred porcelain dolls standing in every inch of the room. Mom was always really weird about her dolls.

"Mom knows every single one of these dolls by name and would know if any one of them was moved an inch." I'm sure Dee believed me, but to take it a step further, I took the glasses off one doll and put them behind her as Mom was walking in. She was all smiles, asking us what we were doing here, surveying the room when she finally saw it. Her eyes folded to a deep slant and a wrinkle formed a V-pattern on her forehead. You could feel the tension come upon the room like a deep wave.

"Where's Suzy's glasses?" She asked in such a serious tone that I could feel DeAnda's heartbeat race twenty paces through the palm of her hand. I didn't mean to frighten her, so I immediately took charge and said, "Oohh, I see them right here. They must have fallen off."

Grabbing the glasses and putting them back, the black cloud of fear instantly dispersed and the childlike smile came across Mom's face again. She walked on through as if nothing had happened.

Dee's face was just in shock. Her jaw dropped wide open and I couldn't help but laugh a little bit. I was used to such a sight, but I could tell that *seeing* things I had told her about was a ton different than just hearing them from my lips.

We stayed there about an hour as well when I started to get a headache, probably from the smell and who knows what kind of toxic things floating around the air in there. I asked Mom where some headache medicine was and she said to look in the cabinet in the bathroom. There was a Tylenol bottle. My body was still adjusting to not having all the drugs I used to take, so I knew two regular, over-the-counter Tylenol wouldn't be strong enough. I took four out of the bottle. A few minutes later, we drove off and about 30 miles down the road, I had figured out those pills were not Tylenol.

I was in trouble.

I went from completely coherent, fun conversation to nodding out, a spinning head and nausea. Dee was asking what was wrong and I tried to play it off as if I was ok, but that girl is way smarter than I gave her credit for. She was ready to rush me to a hospital by the time we reached Tyler city limits. My eyes wouldn't stay in focus and kept rolling back as if a pressure were forcing them. I tried doing everything I could to keep them in focus, even drawing in a journal.

Dee was mad. No, mad is not the word. She was furious. I felt so bad, thinking she was mad at me. She kept reassuring me that it wasn't my fault but Mom's, but I was still trying to defend her. Although I knew Mom had purposely tried poisoning us many times, I was trying to convince Dee (and mostly myself) that this time was an accident. I had to beg her not to call the cops on Mom, and to my surprise, she didn't. I think her main focus was just to help me out.

I blacked out two or three times before we reached her house. She used all her might to help me get up the stairs and into the door of her apartment. I woke up with my head in the bathtub, cold water pouring on it as I was throwing up. I was so embarrassed, but Dee was right there behind me, rubbing my back and telling me it was ok, not to worry—she had me.

My embarrassment waned as I just felt happy to have someone there taking care of me. In the past when things like this happened, I had no one.

The next day I awoke, covered up on her couch, feeling groggy but a lot better than the night before. Those diamond eyes were on the floor, staring at me, making sure I was breathing. She kissed my forehead like tradition and just said, "I'll kiss your lips after you brush your teeth."

We both laughed—a definite welcome sign for the morning with many more to come.

Moving Day

I don't know if Dee and my relationship was intimidating or annoying everyone now, but it was definitely doing something. Our friends were beginning to become bitter toward us, not hanging around as much. We were in our own world anyway, so it didn't affect us much at the time.

A few weeks after the bitterness started, I walked over to Dee's apartment while she was at work to wait for her like I always did, only to find a lot of stuff missing. At first my guess was that they got robbed, but then I saw her roommate packing boxes in her car. Nonchalantly, I asked her what was going on and she simply replied, "Oh, I got a new apartment. When you see her, can you tell Dee the gas and electric will be shut off in a few days?"

She said it with such a coldness that I felt shivers go down my body, cutting the air in the entire house. I thought, of course Dee knew this. She probably just didn't tell me because it wasn't that big of a deal. I sat there and waited for her call, as she always called from work when she was on the way home to make sure I was there.

"Hey, I didn't know y'all were moving?"

She sat on the line with a confused pause, then asked what I was talking about. I proceeded to tell her how half the furniture was gone and that her roommate told me to tell her the electric and gas was about to be shut off. She was in shock, thinking I was joking with her. I had to reassure her a few times that I was being completely serious. She rushed home in a rage, then got on the phone in utter shock at the lack of things around the house. The phone call didn't end well as her roommate, in that same cold tone, said, "Well, I just figured that since you're always with Tim anyway, you'd figure it out and find a place to go." She was so mad; she didn't even give her roommate a proper goodbye—just a proper slam in the ear as she hung up the phone.

I knew I didn't have any answer to give her, but my protective instincts kicked in. "Well, you can stay with us at our house. It will be fine." It subsided her for a bit, and of course, Joey was more than willing to let her stay with us. She actually had a job and a way of contributing.

We started to move things over to my place when we got even more bad news: Joey decided he was fed up with this empty American life and he was moving to Scotland. He would be leaving in the next month, but was going to stay with his

back at "the house on the highway"
with mom & granny

grandparents during that time to save up money for his trip. Neither Dee or me had a place to go.

She decided to pull her last card and go stay with her parents in Quitman. Also on a new journey in their life, they were in the process of packing their house up to move to Missouri. I wondered if things could get any worse...and that's when they did.

Joey moving away and Dee moving a thousand miles away meant that I had only one card left, too: my parents' house in Quitman. I knew this was my time to make a plan of action. I needed to grow up and grow up quick. I was in love and knew, for the next few months, I wouldn't be able to see the girl that I had not spent a day apart from in months.

As the days grew closer to the time everyone was going away, Dee and I spent countless hours with each other at the oddest of places—Mom's house. By now, I was ready to do anything for this girl. After tons of meetings and talks with one of our closest new friends named Holly (who supported us in all of this), she had come up with a plan to live in the TJC dorms when she came back in August. I knew I had to come up with a plan to keep Dee. I wanted to marry her, but was incapable of doing anything to support her.

"While I'm gone, get a GED, learn to drive and find a job. We can work on the rest when I get back."

I was more determined than anything to be a success at all of these. We said our final goodbyes as she got in the car with her Mom and Dad, both with disapproving glances as they drove away. I was determined to prove both of them wrong, and prove to Dee that I could be the man she needed.

This was the beginning of three of the hardest months of my life.

CHAPTER SIX
Another Shift

Good Enough Diploma

The next few months slugged their way by like wax, slowly melting away the days. Nothing would keep my mind occupied enough for me not to get sad that I wasn't seeing Dee every second.

Once a week, I would put all the letters with pictures I had drawn into a box and send it off to Missouri for Dee, to keep her informed on the happenings of me at home without her. Each week I would receive one from her. Hers usually had food and snacks in it to keep me from having to eat every nasty thing that lay around the pathetic excuse of a house where I was staying. We had phone cards to use sparingly. I hid in the back corner of the house, talking on the phone in timed-out, hour-long increments that we always seemed to go over. We would get cut off mid-sentence a lot of times. It would ruin my day until the next time I could scrounge up twenty dollars for another phone card.

Before Dee left, she bought me a final gift from the local bookstore: a GED prep book to get me ready for the test. I had gone through that thing three times, taken both practice tests in the back and now felt ready enough to take it. Mom had finally hidden back enough money (after she had stocked up on the booze needed to cope) and was ready to shell out some to me. I knew I wouldn't be able to wake up without feeling bad if I had to be in Tyler at 7:30 am to take this test, so I just stayed up all night until *Mr. Rogers* starting playing on TV. I knew it was time then, so I woke Mom up for the long trek into Tyler.

She dropped me off at the entrance of the building and I made my way around the maze of hallways until I got to the door marked "GED Testing." I gave my money and sat down as an administrator read out the rules to us one by one, telling the time restraints we would have. I looked around, surprised that I was the youngest looking person in the room of about twelve people. Most looked to be around college age or a little older; some looked like old, grown men.

The guy behind me was about six inches taller and about three feet wider than me, wearing faded overalls covering a green *John Deere* shirt. His mud-stained boots could have fit two of my feet in them and his *Peterbilt* baseball cap matched his giant build. A matted-up beard seemed to muffle and muddle up every word that he said underneath a strong Southern accent.

Three minutes into the test, I hear "Dammit," as the man's pencil broke from pressing too hard on the paper.

Then a few minutes later, "Bullsh—"

"No talking during the test, sir, or we will have to ask you to leave," interrupted the administrator.

I was shaking in my seat, trying not to expose how hard I was laughing on the inside. About ten times over the next few hours, I heard the man quietly saying profanities under his breath about the test. I didn't see what was so hard. All these sections—science, history, language—it all seemed to be pretty self-explanatory. You just read the paragraph and answered the questions asked about what you just read. The only part I didn't know well was the math, but when it came to numbers, I was a pretty good guesser. Plus it was multiple choice, so my chances just went up. It was just like playing the lottery with Mom at the gas station.

Hours passed and we finally finished the test. The man behind me looked like he had just run a marathon.

"So when will I know if I passed or not?"

The lady gave me a reassuring grin and said, "Your GED should be in the mail within a week or two," as if she already knew I had passed or was a psychic. Either way, she was right. The most professional piece of paper I had ever seen my name on arrived in Mom's mailbox within a few weeks. I actually felt proud looking at it.

I was sixteen and had just graduated school. Pretty good accomplishment, considering I had thought I would be dead before I turned sixteen.

State of Texas

Certificate of High School Equivalency

TIMOTHY ANDREW BROOKS

has demonstrated satisfactory performance on the General Educational Development Tests that meets standards prescribed by the Texas Education Agency

Issued: June 7, 2000
Test Version: ENGLISH
Certificate Number: 446574

Commissioner of Education

Getting Ready

Now that I had gotten my GED, I was one step away from getting my act together enough to keep the promise I had made Dee.

I started thinking about what makes good money, looking up things on my friend's computer and asking questions. Computer repair—I could do that and then I could get a job making ten dollars an hour. That would be plenty enough to support a wife, right? I looked into some A+ certification courses online through Tyler Junior College and decided that was what I was going to do. As if by a sign, Mom got a check in the mail for me. It was from my real dad, a child support check.

"You actually get those?"

"No, this is actually the second one I've ever got from him—one when you were two years old and now this one," she said in shock.

I made a deal with her: if she used some of the check to pay for the three courses I needed to take, I wouldn't tell Jerry, and she could keep the rest of the money to do whatever she wanted. She must have thought it was a fair deal because she agreed enthusiastically. I began my courses online a few hours a day at my friend's house down the road.

When I told Dee, she was more than proud of me. She saw me getting my act together and tried to express her joy to her parents who always had a negative rebuttal. I didn't mind though, as long as she was proud of me. I finished all three courses and went to take my final A+ certification test. We drove all the way there to find out that I needed $360 in order to take the test, which was the cost of all three of my courses already and way more than I had—or could come up with.

As I left the testing area with as much defeat as a wounded animal, I walked out to see that Mom was gone. I started walking down the hallway when I saw a familiar old face—an old friend I had met through the Duprees. He told me of his plans to move to Tyler in the next few weeks and asked if I would be interested in staying in an apartment by the college with him and two other guys. Of course I was more than stoked, knowing I would be back in Tyler and Dee would be here as well. A little bit of the discouragement in not taking the test began to fade away as he gave me a ride to the Hobby Lobby where I knew Mom would be.

I went home and told Dee the bad and the good news over the phone. She was always such an encourager, telling me it would all be ok and I would find a different job if I couldn't work fixing computers. She had good news as well—not only was she going to be living on the TJC campus, she was going to be an R.A., residential adviser. This meant she was kind of a dorm mom, but it also meant she would get to live there for free. Her friend, Holly had ended up talking to some people and arranging everything. I was more than excited for her as well. The next few weeks started passing quickly as both of us were getting ready for our reunion and our next move.

Finally, she came to my door, wearing my favorite khaki dress and green bandana, eyes still shining with that special glow. We hugged for days in that moment; I decided I was never going to let her out of my sight again. I had already packed everything she wanted to take to her new dorm into her car, then we got my own suitcase and few belongings. We were off, back to Tyler.

After arranging everything in her room the way she wanted, we went to my new place a few miles down the road. It was a two-bedroom apartment that was going to be shared by four people, my bed being the couch. I didn't mind though. Anywhere that wasn't Mom's was always better—and even better was having Dee so close again.

I was different this time, gone the first day looking for work. By the end of the week I had an interview at JC Penney. They seemed to like my honesty, and I was hired two days later as the stock boy. Dee would give me a ride to work every day, and I would take the bus home if she wasn't around to pick me up.

It was the start of a new chapter in my life, and I was loving it.

i took my job pretty serious...
obvioosly...

A Bad Ride Home

I was getting used to this semi-normal kind of life, going to work from six in the morning until eleven, having the adventure of trying to find a way back to the apartment before lunch. In this time off I would do math in my head, working out schemes on how Dee and I could be married. If I could work more hours, I could make enough, but they only needed me part-time, early in the morning.

I decided to explore more options and began looking for a second job. I applied anywhere that wasn't fast food since that venture didn't go anywhere near how I had planned it. I vowed never to sail that ship again.

Within a week, I was hired at the best of all places for me to work: Toys R Us. Literally, my job was to play with remote-control cars and ride scooters around the store until a customer asked me to find something. Then I would proceed to find any toy their heart desired. It worked out with my schedule perfectly. I would leave JC Penney at eleven and have enough time to walk down the street to Toys R Us and sit in the break room, eating whatever snack Dee had packed for me until I started working the floor at noon.

Now that I was working two jobs, my mind started to get a little crowded and I would end up forgetting to have the proper shirt for each store. JC Penney just required I have a full or semi button top, but the toy store wanted me to have khaki pants and a red top with buttons.

One time in particular I had been rushed for work after sleeping in a bit too long and I forgot my red shirt. I didn't think anything of it until I had gotten to my second job. The manager called me out and told me I wouldn't be able to work the floor or even clock in until I had gone home and changed. I kept dialing from the company phone, but Dee was now in class and all my friends were either at work or in class themselves. Looking desperate and flustered, I decided just to walk the few miles home and get the change of clothes I needed.

Nearby there was an older man who had been listening to all the messages I was leaving for friends. He was probably in his late 60s, early 70s, with metal frame glasses that made his eyes look twice the size they really were. He had light brown suit pants that were slightly above his ankles with a tucked in, button-up Western shirt. Wrinkles marked years of time passed on his forehead. He came up and asked if he could give me ride. I was in such an anxious state that I asked if he was serious and told him I would really appreciate it. We walked outside, got in an older tan car from either the late 70s or 80s, and drove off.

He began telling me how he used to be a young men's mentor through some state program. He said he had mentored hundreds of boys through the years and that a young man in need was always on his radar. That's how he spotted me.

"Are you hungry? I have a tradition that I take all my new friends out to eat at my favorite Mexican restaurant," he said in his jolly, old man tone.

Anyone who knows me knows that I do not turn down free things. And I also don't turn down food. Put them together and I'm sold. Since I didn't have a time given to me to be back at work, I freely gave in. We headed to a very traditional Tex-Mex Tyler restaurant and he began to tell me small stories of some of the guys he'd mentored in the past, telling me that I reminded him a lot of one of the boys.

After we got done and he paid, we headed back in the car and he starts telling me how he's a photographer, loves pictures and loves taking them.

"Would you ever let me take pictures of you?" he said with a half grin. The emptiness in his eyes when he said this sparked something in me. My heart began to race and my eyes tried to focus anywhere but on him.

"I dunno. I'm not really photogenic. I don't like having my picture taken," I said nervously, trying not to give off the impression that I was starting to get scared.

"Well, that's ok. For now. Would you happen to have any pictures of you at your house? Maybe any of you during the summer or while you were swimming?"

His voice tone started to drop and become more serious, less like the jolly old man he had obviously portrayed himself to be. Like a lightbulb clicking on in my head, I realized that if he takes me to my house, he will know exactly where I live. Without sounding too obvious, I started diverting his route to the college campus. As we started to pull up on the one hundred or so dorm rooms where Dee lived, I knew this would be my best bet since guys were not allowed past the lobby. He would have no way of connecting me with any of these girls' dorms.

"Look under your seat and pull out that photo album for me."

We came to a stop in front of the campus.

"Each one of these people are guys like you that I have mentored. I like to keep pictures of all my friends close."

I politely refused and started to open the door to the car. Immediately I was stopped as he slammed the silver door lock shut over my shoulders.

"DON'T LEAVE YET!" he said, now barking. I felt like I was going to throw up and fear built up inside of me so much that I couldn't react. I don't think it crossed my mind that I was probably way stronger and more fit than this old man and could easily take him down. It felt like it always did when an older male figure demeaned me and I shrank like a wilting flower.

"That's better. Now look at my friends. Don't you have any pictures like this?" he said as he turned the first page open. There were boys that didn't look my age, but a lot younger. Every single one had their shirts off. Some had swim trunks on, some just in underwear. As I clumsily strolled through page after page of pictures of the boys, there was a section of just feet. Rows and rows of just boys' feet from the ankle down. I looked confused at this as he said, "Maybe your feet can be in there first, huh? It's beautiful, isn't it?"

"I have to go now. Thanks for the ride," was my answer as I readied for some sort of retaliation. My instincts were right.

"Well, at least give me a hug goodbye."

I don't know if it was the fear or just thinking that it was all I had to give before I could get out of there unharmed, but I obliged and gave him the hug. As if an angel swooped down to save me, I looked over his shoulder as I came in for the embrace and saw a confused look on the most wonderful face I could have asked for at the time. It was DeAnda, driving by in her gold Chrysler LeBaron.

"Oh, my girlfriend…I need to go. Bye!" I yelled. Before he knew what was going on after the shock of my voice being so loud in his ear, I made my way out of the car as fast as I could and was running to her. He had already driven off by the time I made it to Dee's car, breathing as deep as if I had been underwater for too long and lost all my air.

She knew (as she always did) that something was wrong as I started explaining what had happened. She was furious, the same fury in her eyes as when she would hear about all the times Mom would try to harm me. She called my work and the police as well. Work told me to just take the day off and they would see me tomorrow. After a few hours she got my mind off everything that was going on in my head, and finally I was calm enough to be myself again.

I had nightmares all through the night, making the next morning pretty rough. I remembered my red shirt this time at least.

Right around the time I was finishing my first shift, the nightmares birthed reality. I saw the old man again, walking around JC Penney, looking for me. I ran through the back and into the manager's office, told him the situation, and they called the police. Dee was in cautious mode as she was already at the store, picking me up to take me the few blocks down the street. She snuck me out a side entrance of the store and we left, letting the cops escort the man off the property in the other direction.

Since he didn't legally do anything wrong, they couldn't do anything other than tell him that he had to stay at least one hundred yards away from me at all times. Dee was a little upset by this outcome, but I knew one hundred yards would be good enough for me.

No more riding in cars with strangers, I promised as I closed that door of my life.

They're Back

I think people were starting to resent our relationship again because the ones around us were starting to get cold and stopped including us in certain activities. I didn't care though—I loved being engulfed in our own world. Every hour I wasn't working and she wasn't in school, we were together. I would go to her dorm and sit in the lobby with her while she was on duty. Just being in her presence, doing anything, was enough for me.

Holly, her best friend at the time, was also swiftly becoming a sister figure to me. She was filled with something that started a spark in both of us. And the fact that she wasn't resentful of our relationship and still loved us no matter how mushy we were together was a nice quality. She would pray for us and with us with emotions that we deemed to be honest and not cheesy. I knew God (or something) was real, but she actually made that fact a little easier to accept. Not that I would fully take the plunge and believe everything, but I knew there was at least a tinge of reality in the whole religion thing. She was there for any of the problems we were having and listened when we talked about our other friends abandoning us. It felt nice to have someone to vent to.

After a few months of us all growing and getting closer, it felt like our bond was now making it even worse with my other friends. They were starting to become just mean, having dark spirits about them when I would even try to talk. Finally, it got to the point where I was asked to move out. (They told me another guy was coming in to live, and there wouldn't be room for me anymore.) As if the universe told my life it was time to rain down on me, I got fired from my toy store job the same week.

I knew I wouldn't have enough money working one job to pay for a place all by myself. I went to Dee with the dilemma and she went to Holly, who always had an answer. She prayed right there for me, and without any doubt, she told me everything was going to work out—and meant it. The weirdest part was the calmness that came over her and me.

Sure enough, she was right.

The next week my job as a stock boy was coming to an end and the maintenance team at the store was looking for a full-time janitor. I was brought on the next day for training and began my new, full-time job with higher pay. As far as my living arrangement went, Holly was the dorm mother of another girls' dorm on the campus which had a strange room connected to her room and the lobby. She told me that if I kept to myself, I could use that room until I found a proper replacement. It was looking like things were working out.

After a few weeks of staying in this little room and being only one dorm house from my Dee, a funny thing happened. Dee was driving us to get something for lunch, and as she pulled away from the curb, the loudest racket of yelling and screaming came from somewhere unknown. Then we felt the vibration of something hitting her old, gold car. Both of our hearts pounding, we looked out to see two familiar faces. With a bright bluish green, freshly-shaven Mohawk and black-rimmed glasses, Joey's face was grinning and yelling at the window, as was Joshie's, with the same brightly colored hair. We stopped, got out and began hugging like we had just seen a person come back to life.

"I thought you were in Scotland!" we screamed in unison.

"I got deported!" he said as he laughed and explained the situation of him not having a return ticket. The country frowned on that, let him stay for a few weeks, and shipped him back home. He was starting his job back in a week and moving to Tyler.

I told him about my recent success as a janitor and how I had kind of gotten kicked out. Without hesitation, he asked me to come live with him and Joshie in the new apartment they were getting. I was stoked out of my mind, mainly because I respected Holly so much; I didn't want her to get in trouble for secretly boarding me in her dorm room. Me being a bit of a scatterbrain, I had almost let it slip numerous times in front of the wrong people. I was also excited to be thrown back into a similar situation, but this time having a way to support myself and not be such a burden.

We ended up hanging out the rest of the day before they drove back to Mineola where Joey was temporarily staying for the next week until they got moved back. We told Holly the good news, and as if she had been expecting it, she said, "I told you everything was going to work out."

The next week passed and we gathered everything I had and moved it over to the new house. It was another brick quadplex, only a block away from where we had been living previously. It was upstairs, and as you walked into the corridor, you could immediately smell weed pouring from the adjacent apartment. Not bad, I thought, as old memories came rushing back. It was a little different than before as I didn't crave it, but just enjoyed the scent.

The first things I saw inside were a living room with lots of windows and old, musty carpet. The smell wasn't the greatest, but it also wasn't the worst thing I had ever smelled—kind of like if a dog smoked and lived alone as a bachelor. There was a large, square-shaped closet that Joshie had already claimed as his, and further down, two adjacent bedrooms separated by an old, tile-floored bathroom. Joey had already set up his things in the larger bedroom, so I assumed the other one was mine.

It was incredible.

I had two wooden windows, a small closet and a door that shut. This was the first room I had that was my own. We both sat the few things we had on the floor as I took it all in. I didn't have a bed, but Joey had an old cot that he had gotten from his grandparents. I unfolded it and set it up in the corner. We spent the night dressing the room in pictures I had kept in my tiny vintage suitcase over the years.

This new chapter was off to a good start, and I couldn't wait to see how it progressed.

CHAPTER SEVEN
Crowded House

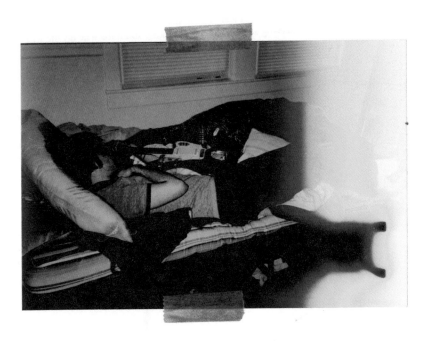

Harmony & Understanding

Things were settling in at the new place and it was just like old times, minus all the drugs. I would either see Dee in the morning time when she dropped me off for work or in the early afternoon when she picked me up as I still couldn't drive. I tried a few times with failure; my fear wouldn't let me leave the parking lot. It was ok for Dee though. She never complained once about having to spend time taking me everywhere, and I didn't mind the company.

As a theatre major, Dee was gaining more and more school activities. One in particular was the most fun, for me if not for her. It was a song and dance group called Harmony & Understanding. After months of rehearsals, with me hearing about them and even going to the end of a few, they had their first big performance. I had gotten to know the director of the group by now, and she had come to accept my quirkiness. She said I could come to the performance and hang out only if I would dress in the proper attire.

The most proper I had ever been in my life was when I went to my job interviews and that had just consisted of wearing khakis and a tucked-in polo shirt. Luckily Joey and I wore the same size clothes, and he had a Blues Brothers suit that I was able to borrow. I put the suit on and had him tie a tie around my neck. It was the most important I had felt in my life up to that point. Although I felt important, I didn't feel that the suit fit the way I felt about myself on the inside. It made me feel undeserving at the same time, thinking about the way my life was heading.

When Dee pulled up to the door to get me, that feeling sank in even deeper. She was beautiful—beyond beautiful. It was as if reality hit me like a car wreck. What was she doing with me? Her eyes were sparkling in the same fashion they always had, but now she had a red dress with the same sparkles all over it. It was the first time I had seen her all dolled up and I was at a loss for words. She giggled nervously at the way I was gawking at her and said, "I'm sorry. I know you don't like it. I look ridiculous with all this makeup on and everything, but it's just for stage performance." She barely got that last part out before I cut in and told her the complete opposite. She was stunning and I couldn't take my eyes off her. I told her my insecurities and like a glove, her words of comfort fit nicely around me, waning all those feelings away...or at least suppressing them for the time being.

I sat on the front row, smiling ear to ear the entire performance, so proud I could have busted down and started crying right there. Maybe I was just being too sensitive or maybe it was just her love being so thick—it was tearing into me, exposing how I truly felt. Either way, at every single performance from then on, you could find me on the front row just as proud, goofy grin from ear to ear, cheering on the girl I loved.

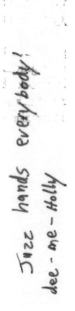

Jazz hands everybody!
dee - me - Holly

Mall Friends

Working in the mall full-time meant that I had ample time to become a mallrat on my hour-long lunch breaks. I usually wouldn't really eat more than a snack before heading off down the long corridors to people watch, always one of my favorite things.

Over a few weeks I kept noticing a girl working at the sunglasses stand in a middle kiosk, and she was noticing me as well. It wasn't the same kind of notice that a girl has in hopes that the boy will look back and sweep her off her feet. It was different... more of a do-I-know-you-from-somewhere-and-if-not-can-we-be-friends, notice. Finally, after weeks of passing each other in the mall and giving friendly smiles back and forth, she stopped me.

"Hey, why do you always carry your backpack around with you?" she asked from over the counter.

I kinda laughed at her boldness and just replied back with ease, "It's my comfort, I guess. I really don't like being without it."

"Yeah, me neither. I'm Jessie. Which one of these stores do you work at?"

I began to tell her, and our first conversation started to unfold. We were talking about music and life and our significant others and before I knew it, my lunch break was coming to a close. We said our goodbyes and I told her that I would come back tomorrow if she was around then. We seemed to always have the same work schedule, so it worked out pretty well.

Our friendship grew and pretty soon she was becoming more like family. We even introduced each other to our friends as brother and sister. I loved the idea of having a sister in my life—especially with my relationship with Dee growing more and more. I needed another female voice to bounce ideas off of so I could see if the plans I was making for Dee would be appreciated. I always loved surprising her with things, so Jessie was a good filter.

Dee still had not met her yet, but she heard enough about her from me. I could tell there was never an ounce of jealousy from her because we knew each other's hearts so well. There was never any need for it. They would meet soon enough.

Another friend I made in the mall was a jeweler. I met him when asking around about custom rings at the different jewelry stores in the mall. I knew Dee and I were not the traditional type of people, so we couldn't have any typical ring. Also, my budget wouldn't have enough for anything other than a special ring...and by special, I mean as cheap as I could possibly get.

We were both still determined to get married, and I never knew when the right time would be, but I knew getting a ring was a key start. With the help of Holly and Jessie, I was able to get down a basic idea of having matching silver bands with indented stars surrounding the circle.

My jeweler was not a fan of some of the people he worked with, so he gave me his personal number in order to work with me "off the clock." That made me happier since those people were a little intimidating to me anyway. We talked over a few phone calls, and I made some visits to his house to concept out the rings. Dee had two necklaces she had gotten from her grandmother, and I had gotten it out of her that whenever we did get rings, she wanted them to be put into the bands. By this time, I had already snuck said necklaces out and the plans were in order.

Now it was just a waiting game on when the bands would be done...and when I would officially pop the question.

Jessie became part of our disfunctional family

September 23, 2000

Palms sweaty, heart beating out of my chest, my nerves bolting from each vein all the way to the top of my head, making it hard to breathe—something about making it official scared me to death.

Tonight was going to be the night.

I had picked up the ring from the jeweler's house, grabbed Holly's guitar and was waiting nervously by the door for Dee to get there. I didn't tell her what we were doing, only to wear my favorite outfit. I had a special night planned for her.

She pulled up and I lost my breath. She looked like an angel from head to toe with sparkles dancing from her eyes as they met mine. We drove to the park, much like we had before, but this time there was an electric tinge to the air that felt as if it were petrifying me.

As we pulled the car over, I grabbed the guitar and Dee grabbed the blanket. We set off for the centermost tree in the park. The tension began to fade enough for me to get some small talk out as we were setting up our special spot in the grass. The sun was just beginning to fade out in dark amber and pink waves behind the glint of Dee's eyes. I clumsily pulled out the guitar and told her that I had something special to sing for her.

I think it came as a surprise because I was always so shy about my musical abilities. She didn't even know that I played the guitar until a few months after we started dating. I had spent the last few months writing and practicing for this moment, but I felt the build of emotion start creeping into my eyes. I was almost too choked up to get the entire mess of a song out.

The best part about Dee is that she could see the meaning and the love I had for her in those few moments as I stumbled through the song I had written for her; she couldn't have cared less if there were bad notes or missed chords. She cried with me and told me she loved me. I could tell in her embrace she felt the same way.

As I regained sight, I leaned over and grabbed a plastic sphere like you get from a twenty-five cent gumball machine and handed it to Dee, holding both her hands around the ball as I spoke these words.

"I know I have not had a lot of things go right in my life, and I'm not sure about a lot of things in my life, but the one thing I am sure of is my love for you. I want to start making things right and prove the world wrong with you. Will you be my bride?"

These were some of the hardest words to ever come out of my mouth. Not because I didn't mean them or hold truth behind them, but because all of my life, I had not known anything but rejection. Even though I knew deep down that Dee felt the same for me, there was this feeling of being exposed to the core. The seconds after seemed like hours as I craned to hear and see her reaction.

There were tears, a huge embrace and a kiss that immediately cured any and all doubts, weeding out all my nervous thoughts.

"Of course, I will be your bride. I've always been your bride," she said under the joyful tears falling slowly from her diamond eyes. She looked down and opened the plastic round container to find the head of a white daisy. Inside the yellow center of the flower was a silver ring with stars indented all around it, just like we had talk-ed about. As she saw it, the tears began to flow again. After a second embrace, I grabbed her little, delicate hand and placed the ring gently on her finger. She got up and started yelling and running and doing cartwheels as if she had been caged for years and had finally broken free.

"I'm getting married—yeaaah!!! I'm getting married!!!!" Anyone within a mile radius could hear her screaming in joy.

"Engagement photos!! Let's go!" she yelled last, grabbing up our things and heading for the car. This was why I needed her—I forget about these little things.

We went to the nearest drug store and grabbed a disposable Polaroid camera, then drove back to the same spot. Not having someone there to take pictures made half the shots come out blurry, but neither one of us seemed to mind. We were just basking in the moment and taking it all in. There was nothing that could stop us now. I was promised to her and her to me forever.

How could things get any better?

my diamond eyed girl - Engagement photos

Late For Work

It had been a few months since we had gotten engaged and for us, things couldn't be more amazing.

The same couldn't be said for Dee's parents though.

Every time Dee tried to talk to her mom about it, they just ended up getting in a fight—and don't even *try* talking to her dad. I guess they had hoped for much better for their daughter. I couldn't drive, didn't finish high school, was an ex-druggie and worked as a janitor at a clothing store.

Mom—it didn't make a difference to her. With he drugs and alcohol she was on mixed with her schizophrenia, she barely even knew who I was. Even with all that, at this point, I would gladly have accepted a visit to her house over a visit to the opposite side. I could tell the negativity coming from her parents was a strain on Dee's mind and heart. She just wanted them to see what she saw. That took some convincing even for me to see sometimes, so I never took it too harshly. It was what it was, and I wasn't planning on changing my vow to prove the world wrong.

One morning, as normal as any other morning that Dee took me to work, we were talking. We had made plans to take our first real getaway together. Not too far, but for us, it was a first. We had decided to take $100, rent a car and drive down to Austin to see one of our favorite pop-punk bands.

As we were pulling up, she said, "So...what are we gonna do while we're in Austin besides see The Impossibles? It's my birthday weekend."

I, being the goof that I was, said as matter-of-factly as I could, "Well, duh—we're gonna get married." I said it with so much authority that I even shocked myself.

The car was silent now.

"Really?" was the next word to flow out of Dee's mouth, curiously awaiting my answer.

"Well...why not? What are we waiting for anyway? To be financially stable? For your parents' approval? Like that will ever happen...This is as good a time as any, isn't it?" We both smiled really big as I continued. "Driveee! We have a marriage license to get!"

And we laughed like little kids and drove to the courthouse.

When we got there, I was being dumb, saying things like, "It's ok for brother and sister to get married, right? That's legal now, ain't it?" The clerk wasn't that impressed; she didn't know whether to believe me or not.

"You two sure you aren't related?" the clerk honestly asked as Dee gave me a playful slap on my shoulder.

"Be serious for a second." Dee's tone firmed up as it would when I was starting to cross the line.

I managed to slack off from being the funny man for a few more minutes until all the documents were finally done and we were holding them in our excited little hands. I managed to get to work just an hour late, but explained to my boss that I would work through lunch to make it up. I told him the circumstances—I was held up in court, a valid excuse and a truthful one, even if I didn't explain exactly what I was doing at court.

I was so excited I had to tell someone. Since I had such a good excuse for being late, my boss didn't make me hold up my end of the deal by skipping lunch, which I was thankful for. I rushed out to the sunglasses stand to see Jessie. I must've had a grin from ear to ear because she immediately knew something was up.

"I have a secr—," and before I could finish, she cut me off.

"You're getting married this weekend, aren't you?" She already knew we were making a trip to Austin.

"How in the world did you know that?" I let out in utter shock, kind of laughing about it.

"Sisters just know these things. Plus your face gave it away when I saw you from five stores down the hallway," she said, laughing. She gave me a huge hug and congratulated me. It felt good to have at least one other person to share the experience.

Dee picked me up after work and she had been wearing that same grin all day too. I could tell we were glowing.

Wedding Day

Plans were underway. Some secret, some surprises, some known, but so exciting that it made me lose my breath with every thought.

We had packed for our weekend getaway, stopped by the rent-a-car and gotten our '99 Pontiac Grand Prix. It was bright red and filled to the top with gas, ready for our next chapter of life. Dee would be doing all the driving as I still had never gotten over the fear of...well, everything that was outside of the car and being in control of not running into those things. She didn't mind a bit.

It was March 3rd, Dee's twenty-first birthday. I had already given her a gift—as if our wedding wouldn't be enough of a gift in itself. Holly and I, along with a few of her friends, had all chipped in to get her the blue acoustic guitar she always played at the local music store. As cool as it was, nothing could compare to the fact that, by the end of the weekend, we would be married.

We knew of a local Church Under The Bridge and were planning on just going to the service on Sunday, then asking the pastor if he would marry us. However, before that took place, we were able to contact an old friend of Dee's. His dad was the pastor of a church she went to while growing up in Mineola, and it just so turned out that he had been ordained as a minister as well. It looked as if things would start going smoothly now.

As far as the trip down, it did, but then things started to get a little complicated.

It was night by the time we got to the old friend's house. They welcomed us warmly into their apartment and started conversing with us. We told them why we were eloping and how much we loved each other, that we didn't want to spend another day not joined as one. He heard the sincerity in our voices and our plans, but then threw us a curve ball; he wanted Dee's parents' approval before he would marry us. The brokenness started to show in Dee's eyes at that statement, knowing she would never receive even an ounce of blessing. She expected the worst—and got it.

On the phone with her mom, I could see the struggle Dee was having to convince her that she was doing the right thing. Her mom was explaining that this would be one of the biggest mistakes of her life, calmly but sternly giving Dee all the warnings and concerns she had. Dee was keeping it together pretty well, aside from the tears welling up slowly from the corners of her eyes. Then in the background, loud enough to break through the silent tension in the bedroom where she was, I heard Dee's dad barking at her.

"IF YOU MARRY THAT BOY I WILL DISOWN YOU!!!"

Dee lost every ounce of fighting back her emotions at those words and exploded with tears, laid the phone down and walked away. Into the arms of the wife of a pastor who couldn't possibly want to marry us, Dee went sobbing. The pastor picked up the phone she had laid down to hear the last few choice words her dad was barking through the line and tried his best to calm him down. Her dad wasn't having it—told him he was an idiot if he married us, then slammed the phone in his ear.

Emotions filled the air to the point of thickness that if there wasn't a voice of reason in the room, Dee or I would have both drowned right there. It felt like all the breath had been knocked out of us, and we were just waiting on someone to finish us off.

The young pastor stood up in the room and said, "I don't care what they think. I prayed about it, and I have peace. I can see the love in both of your eyes. I have faith in you two. Let's go get you married."

Our tears turned from the sludgy, dark, depressing kind to those filled with joy. They were weightless, seeming to float off our faces, cleaning the worries we once had. I realized I had forgotten to get a nice, white shirt to go along with the black pants and suit coat I had bought from a thrift store a few days ago, so the pastor grabbed one from his closet with safety pins in place where the cufflinks would have been. It was perfect. I waited around twenty minutes while Dee got dressed and ready. When she came out, she was perfection.

Her hair was shining with a flower wreath intertwined in between each lock—a crown fit for a queen. Her peach and cream dress flowed as if it were a waterfall of fabric that just surrounded her body as she walked. Holly had managed to turn her granny's nightgown into a gorgeous fairy gown hypnotizing to the eyes. Those diamond eyes sparkled as we locked glances with each other and drank in the moment.

Drunk from the reality of what was about to happen, I think we must have floated to the car while the pastor and his family gathered things from the house, packing their son in the car in front of us. We pulled up to a small lake with a restful park area to the side, and as we stood there holding hands, the pastor's wife and sister started lighting the Catholic glass candles with pictures of Jesus and Mother Mary in a circle around us. The wife grabbed a camera almost double her size and began filming as he started the short, impromptu ceremony.

I was shaking, voice cracking, my nerves were on fire with excitement, and I could feel the same pulse from Dee's hands as well. She looked down and saw I was still holding a plastic toy rabbit belonging to the pastor's kid; I hadn't even noticed I had it. We both laughed and shook a little bit from nerves. We said our vows and love for each other clumsily, maybe not even getting out the words that we wanted to, but both knew what we were trying to say on the inside. Our souls were interlocked in a conversation that our mouths couldn't comprehend. That's all that mattered.

After a few short minutes and a prayer, he said the words we had waited to hear.

"By the State of Texas, I now pronounce you man and wife. You may kiss the bride."

And that I did, followed with the most sincere embrace I had ever experienced.

As if it had been planned the whole time, a boat with Christmas lights streamed all across it floated by as we were holding each other, the people on it cheering for us with enthusiasm. That was the moment I felt our bodies completely join each other. Our eyes teared up again and we began thanking the pastor for making all of this possible, hugging him and his family.

"Now get out of here, you two! Go enjoy a blessed married life together!" were the parting words as we drove to the venue for the punk show we had originally come to see before the whole wedding idea. We went straight there in our wedding clothes and converse and arrived just in time to see one of the singers right before he went on; he asked what the occasion was. When we told him we had just gotten married, he congratulated us and said it was an honor for us to be there on our wedding night. When they went on, they changed their signature opening lines just for us.

"Hi! We're The Impossibles and our friends, Tim and DeAnda, just got married!" The show went on and after almost every song; he made a toast to us, or told the crowd to give a high five if we were near them. The whole night was a big celebration with people we didn't know, hugging us and high-fiving and congratulating. It as the best reception we could ever have asked for...even though it wasn't catered. We decided the first food place we saw was going to be our wedding cake. There was a Mexican food cart just outside the venue called "Bad Ass Fajitas" and you better believe that was our cake.

After we danced it up and had the night of our life, we decided it was time to find a place to sleep for the night, so we went back to the garage where our rental was parked. It wasn't there. In a panic, we both expected the worst. Just as we were beginning to let it bring down the spirit of where we had just been, I ran up one floor in the garage and saw it parked in the same spot we had left it.

"I guess our minds were a little preoccupied when we parked here, " Dee said with a laugh. It was a perfect ending to a perfect night as we found a nice hotel a few blocks away and settled in.

The next day we made the most of our honeymoon as we went to Waterloo records and gave each other $50 to spend on whatever we wanted as "wedding gifts." All in all, our entire wedding cost a grand total of $300—$100 for the rental car, $100 for the hotel, and $100 on CDs and band posters.

I wouldn't have changed one thing about it...the perfect start to the rest of our lives.

The Aftermath

We came back to our lives as if nothing had changed...but everything had. What once was two people was now one, and it felt like we were a team about to conquer the world. Now we were living in the same house. We were both so proud to tell everyone as we made our rounds that afternoon, visiting different people.

The first people we saw were Joey and his girlfriend. They gave us a huge congratulatory hug and we felt the excitement for us in their voices.

One particular person we visited probably couldn't have cared less at the time— Mom. She was having another stint inside the mental rehabilitation center, as I found out from Granny, so we thought...why not go see her?

We had to sign in, remove any objects that could be used as weapons and leave them at the front desk. Somehow they let us take our huge video camera (like the kind you hoist on your shoulder) back there. I'm sure that violates some kind of code, but nevertheless, we took it to show Mom the video of us getting married. We passed by a few of the residents, some completely normal except for maybe a minor twitch here and there. Others were full-blown screaming, others laughing or crying in their places as we walked by. Mom was plopped down in a stained, green fabric chair from the 80s, watching a big, box console TV.

"Hey Mom, " I said as she looked at me, confused at why I was calling her Mom.

"I'm too young to have kids," was her response. I knew she was "flipped out" and this visit was basically pointless, but I proceeded to try and convince her of who I was and show her the video. She still wasn't grasping the reality yet, but she kept saying "Hey, these are my kids. They just got married!" to everyone around her. We kind of laughed awkwardly at the situation, hoping for it to dissipate soon.

One of the other residents, a hunched-over lady with curly, scraggily hair and jagged, worn-down teeth came up to us as we were watching the replay of our marriage.

"He doesn't love you. They didn't invite you to the wedding. He doesn't love you!" she said through gnarled teeth. At that a resident nurse came over and ushered her away, telling us that time was up and we needed to leave.

"Couldn't she have come sooner?" I said with a half nervous laugh. Dee smiled and we packed up and walked out.

As I was getting in the car, Dee just leaned in and said, "I'm sorry." I was confused at what she was sorry about at the time, but I accepted it. Somehow it made me feel better even though I didn't realize I was hurt and needed it.

The rest of our visits went off a little smoother, minus the fact that Dee's parents hadn't accepted the fact, and as far as we knew, never would. For that, I gave the same "I'm sorry" back to Dee. She assured me everything was going to be ok now.

No More Room

Things were going so smoothly.

I had gotten a raise in my job. I was starting to pick up more spiritual guidance from church. Our marriage relationship was growing steadily. Heck, we had even upgraded from the fold-out cot to a real bed. It was Mom's from when she was a kid, given to me by Granny, but still... it was a bed.

I guess the only downfall was our living space and not having the privacy that newly-weds require. There was always someone living in our house. Once there were two deaf people living in the closet for a month, then when they moved out, a South Korean kid. After that Joshie turned it into a hibernation den. Finally, Holly moved in. So in all, it was me, Dee, Holly, Joey and his girlfriend all living in a tiny, two-bedroom apartment. It was way past time to go, so we told Joey we would be looking for a place of our own soon and went to searching.

After doing the math and checking a few places, we finally found an upstairs, one-bedroom efficiency apartment that we could afford. We put in our deposit and got our key.

As we walked into the small, empty space, we didn't feel the quaintness of it. We sat in the floor of the living room in awe that we had done it—we had a place of our own.

It was perfect.

We got help from friends to move every-thing in, including our purple velvet couch with a missing leg that we substituted with old books. We spent the entire night hanging posters and setting up. Finally, we were done turning the empty space into our home.

We sat snuggled together and watched Peter Pan, or part of it, before we both fell asleep, exhausted from the move but excited to see what lay ahead for us in the future.

we have always been "the weird one"

CHAPTER EIGHT
The Apartment

Driving Now

We had been settled into our new apartment for about a month or two now and were really getting the hang of it.

Dee had started working as a barista and I actually switched from being a janitor to a warehouse worker. It was a nice change, but also very isolated as the store was about five miles from the warehouse where I now worked. With our more complicated schedules and Dee still going to school fulltime, she thought it was probably the appropriate time to start learning how to drive. Although I was scared to death, she had complete confidence in me as I rounded the parking lot a few hundred times. She thought I was ready after a few weeks, so we took a trip down to the DMV.

I didn't know there would be a written test, but I guessed at most of the answers as logically as I could. It wasn't enough on the first two tests because I bombed them, but luckily the third was a lot easier and different. Maybe they just feel sorry for people who fail twice, but I finally ended up getting a high enough score to take the second part of the test, the driving part. I had that down; the main thing I was worried about was the parallel parking section. The funny part is that the space I needed to park in could have fit a large school bus. All I had to do to pass was get it in between those lines. Even the instructor could tell it was a joke and he kinda smiled at me when he saw my face in shock at the simplicity of the task at hand. As I rolled back in to the parking spot, the instructor shook my hand and told me to go inside to get my picture taken and my temporary license.

"What? I failed? What did I do wrong?" He looked at me, confused, as I continued. "Temporary? How long until I can get a real license?"

He then started laughing at me. "You're as confused as a little puppy, aren't you? Temporary...meaning your real license has to be printed and sent to you in the mail."

My face shrunk back down to a more relaxed state and I said, "Yeah, yeah, of course. I knew that," then ran out of the car to get my final piece of the puzzle. A few months late, but still...it's the thought that counts, right?

Australia...Nevermind

Dee was starting to make new, scholarly friends from working at the cafe in the bookstore. It was cool how we would always meet someone new individually, then introduce the same people each other as our new friends. It was fun learning new things from different types of people.

One in particular we were growing to know more and more. She had started coming to the house to watch movies, just hang out and talk. We really enjoyed having her around. She told us the sad but exciting news of her impending move to Australia for school. The best part was that she would be living there for free through scholarships and grants.

Dee piped in like she occasionally does with, "I wanna do that. Can I go?" It came as a surprise to me, and I let out a little laugh. It was even more of a surprise as our friend piped up and said, "Of course you can go! I can help get paperwork and grants for both of you."

This started a two-hour discussion, excitement whirling around in our heads as they got me on board with the idea. By this time, Dee's mom had become a little less wary of our marriage, so Dee got on the phone the next day to tell her about our new plans. She wasn't too happy about it and I'm sure her dad was against the idea even more. He still wasn't on par with us being married yet, but I figured, give it a little time and things would settle.

After about an hour of her mom telling her she wasn't sure about her being so far away and Dee trying to reassure her like she always had, the conversation ended. I didn't even have to ask how it went, and Dee knew it. She just said, "About as expected, but I still haven't changed my mind."

We both laughed as we lay in bed and daydreamed about moving a million miles across the world. We planned on leaving in January and just barely had two months to plan everything, as it was already November.

The next day, I went to work and did my normal stock boy/warehouse odd jobs, but I didn't see anyone. Finally, after thirty minutes or so of work, I saw everyone having a private meeting in a back office without me. I didn't think anything of it, just went about my day as normal until it was time to clock out. I cleaned up around the house and worked on music a little bit as I waited for Dee to get home from work. She came in the door half nervous and scared in her eyes.

"What's wrong? Are you ok?" I asked, leaning in to grab her purse and plastic pharmacy bag.

"I think I'm pregnant," she said with tears of fear welling up in her eyes.

"Whoa...that's awesome...right?" I questioned, not fully grasping the weight of her words. I went with her to the bathroom as we waited on the results.

"Two lines—no? Plus sign—yes?" She took a look first, saw the results and began weeping. They were not tears of disappointment, but more of anxiety and fear. I knew she needed reassurance as I hugged her.

"This is amazing!!! We're going to have a little me or you!! We can do this!!" After the shock of it all wore off, the reality started setting in.

Wow. I'm going to be a dad. I don't know how to be a dad, except for what I've seen in movies or seen Boyd do.

We both sat, half daydreaming, then each would chime in with a sentence to break the tension and make each other laugh. She got on the phone at two in the morning to call her mom.

"Mom...we're not going to Australia anymore." There was a pause.

"You called this late at night to tell me that?"

"No, there's something else...I'm going to have a baby. I'm pregnant."

After a long pause to contemplate the words her mom just took in, she responded, "Are you serious?!! I'm so happy for you!" You could tell she meant those words,

Nothing thats just right ever
works. Happiness is a diesese
that makes life complicated Noone
understands or maybe they do they just
dont admit it. well Im still
alive I Guess thats a start. But
whats life anyway. Its a mass
void of endless disapointments that
could've been avoided If I didn't have
this ounce of hope that something good
would happen to me. I need something I
can never have. oh well I guess we
all need something...

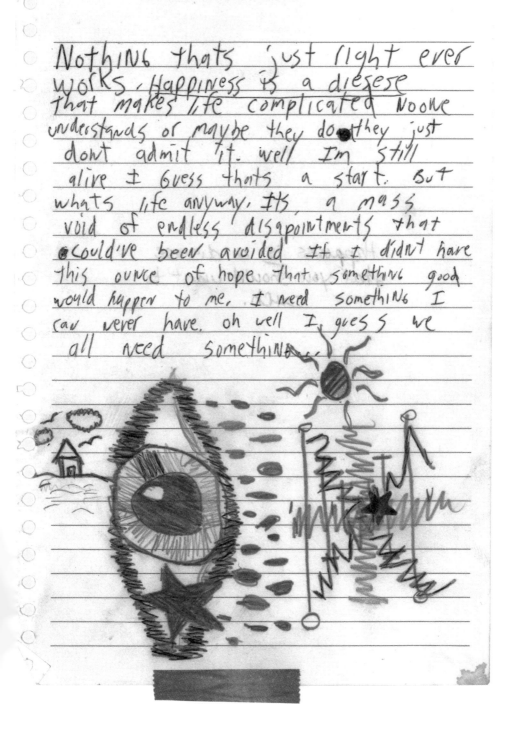

125

because the tears in Dee's eyes didn't lie. The excitement her mom had for Dee meant more than she ever knew. We finally got to sleep for a few hours that night before I had to head to work.

I was excited to share my good news with everyone, but before I got a chance, I was ushered into the same office where everyone had been the day before. This time it was just me, the main boss, and the warehouse boss.

"Tim, we are shutting down the warehouse and consolidating it back to the main store."

"Oh. Ok. Do you want me to drive to the main store from now on?" I asked naively.

"No, we're saying there won't be room for you at the main store—it will already be packed with people. I'm sorry, but we are going to have to let you go."

My heart sunk to the deepest part of my chest. Why now? A baby on the way and instead of going to work to share the good news, I would be heading home to tell Dee the bad news. It was the longest ride home I had taken in a long time.

As I got in the door to see Dee, confused at what I was doing home, I broke the news to her. We both started crying, but as she hugged me, I didn't feel sorry for myself. I felt the strength and willpower to find a way to provide for the family that was on its way. My family. I told her, "We will get through this," and we both knew I meant it this time.

Desperate, I started to pray. Although I still wasn't 100% (or even close) to fully trusting in the God idea, I knew that Dee did, and I was trying my best.

New Job

It wasn't long before I found a new job, a profession even. One of the scholarly friends we met at the bookstore had family that owned a window cleaning company. He set me up with an interview in the following days. It was one of the weirdest interviews I had ever been to...not that I had been to a lot, but this one was at the boss's house.

He asked me to invite my wife along as well. It felt as if it was more of a therapy session and reminded me a lot of when the CPS people would come over to our house to talk to us kids. Asking a lot of personal questions and very few actual skill and previous job questions, they even went so far as to ask questions about my parents.

"Well, I only have a mom really. I never knew who my dad was," I said.

The boss's wife chimed in with, "Oh, so you're from a broken home?"

"Well, yeah...I guess a lot of it was broken, but that's just 'cause we always lived in older homes," I said dumbly. I had never heard the term "broken home".

Dee later explained to me what it meant and I didn't understand why it was called a "broken" home. There was no other way I could see it, and it seemed to work for me, right? I still wasn't completely used to a lot of the things in my past being weird, even though Dee had been trying to explain it to me for a long time now. Maybe it was a blocking mechanism I used to maintain, a shell that hadn't been broken yet.

A few days after the interview, I got a call back from the boss asking if I could start work Monday at 5:30 am. Of course, I jumped at the opportunity and launched my new career. I guess the boss took the broken home thing to heart as he played the role of strict father as he was teaching me how to spread water and soap on a window. It didn't seem like rocket science to me, but apparently there's a lot more to it than meets the eye.

I didn't like one second of the training I was going through, or the long, eight to ten hour days I started working. I knew I had to be a provider though, so I tried my best not to complain to Dee when I came home and keep my frustrations bottled up—another coping skill I had learned growing up. She could read me too well by then, but she, getting more and more pregnant, didn't have the energy to pull it out of me. She figured I would let it out when I needed.

"The smile on my face isn't always real..." Lyrics from my music idol were kinda my motto. If it looks good on the outside, people will think you feel good on the inside.

I guess it only goes so far though.

The Piano

As life started flying by, I was getting used to eating with Dee every time the baby was hungry and gaining weight right along with her. Life was feeling comfortable.

It was nearing Christmas and I wanted to get Dee something that mattered, even though we were saving money...or at least trying to. I had to come up with something great. A piano—in an upstairs apartment, of course—that's a great idea!

Mom had given her old piano to me a long time ago when I used to take lessons. It had a cool background story. Grandpa had bought it to learn how to play a song for Granny to win her over. She said the piano playing could use some work, but the guy behind the keys would do just fine. That was the end of his music career, but they ended up passing it down to Mom, then she to me.

I grabbed my friend with a truck and two of the scrawniest, nimble people I knew and headed down to pick it up. Loading it was not a problem, and the forty-mile ride back with us slamming the keys, serenading everyone we could was entertaining as well. Then the fact set in that we were going to have to get this thing up about twenty or more stairs and maneuver it into my little apartment. All this had to be done before Dee got off work, since it was supposed to be a surprise for her.

I was at the front, the one big friend I had was on the back with all the weight, and the two scrawny friends were on either side, looking and acting like they were helping. After fifteen minutes of grunts and heaves, we finally made it to the top and celebrated for a second before we squeezed and pushed it through the doorway, finally placing it in the corner of the room. Looking back, I don't know how it didn't bust through the floor, but at the time, it never even crossed my mind.

Phase One was over. No, I couldn't just give Dee an old piano with a cool story—I had to take it one step further and decoupage it with pictures of the Beatles. For that I enlisted a few of my more crafty girlfriends and we all hurriedly cut and glued pictures to the entire surface of the piano. It was about seventy-five percent done when I had to go pick up Dee, so I quickly devised a plan to go to the store on the way home and buy a few things to eat. It bought me a good twenty minutes of extra time, just enough for the girls to completely finish.

She walked into the house; surprised to see friends there...and then her eyes met the piano.

"Oh my gosh!! I knew something was weird—you never take that long picking out food!" she said in a surprised laugh.

She loved it and I had achieved the face for which I was hoping. I played a few tunes for her and then we just sat at the bench, looking and admiring all the work that had been put into the project and the history in the keys.

Christmas 2001

An Extra Bedroom

Getting things ready for a baby, we started to run out of space to put everything. Our quaint bedroom barely fit our bed as it was, and now we had a crib and a closet full of diapers and wipes, gidgets and gadgets that I had no clue about how they worked. We checked our budget again and knew that we had to make a way to get a bigger place.

The manager at our apartment said that if we upgraded to a two bedroom, we could get the first month free. If you know me by now, when someone says "free," I'm all over it. It was settled—we were going to be making the huge move from one side of the complex to the other.

Dee did what she could, being seven months pregnant and for some reason, getting sicker every month as the pregnancy progressed. Even packing boxes looked as if it were taking a toll on her body, so I had to all but force her to stay lying down.

She's stubborn and a fighter about being lazy though, so that was definitely an ongoing battle. I knew I would need help after a week of packing things up and Dee finally submitting to my requests of just resting, so I called a mover. I know the idea of hiring a moving company to move from one side of a building to the other is redundant, but I had that huge piano in there (and I found a good deal on the movers). That's one less stress off my plate. I got them to move the bedroom section first so Dee could just lie down while they moved in the rest.

It was exciting to have a new place, but the excitement was short-lived since I was mostly worrying about Dee and why she felt so bad. My faith was at the highest it had been in my life so far, and even though I didn't totally understand it, I knew that praying helped. I just prayed for wisdom on how to be her protector. How could I make her feel better in this time when we were both confused about why she was hurting so much? It didn't seem like my prayer worked this time, but I think He took it into account and helped me later...like He didn't want me to expect to ask for things and just receive them right then, like a spoiled child. But that's exactly how I felt.

A few months after we had gotten all settled into our new two-bedroom, we got a few extra things for the house, one being a bunk bed. On occasion, we would sleep in that second bedroom. I had blacked out the window with aluminum foil so it was dark at all times—pitch black, so if Dee needed to take a nap during the middle of the day or if she wanted to sleep in, it would be a possibility.

One night as we were in there, I was in deep REM sleep and saw a huge flash of light—almost like lightning was striking my dream. I jolted awake. When I awoke, I was sitting straight up like I had never even fallen asleep, and I felt something warm against me. In the darkness, I started to come back to reality; I realized the warm feeling was Dee—I was holding her, carrying the weight of her entire body against me. She was crying.

"How did you do that? I was falling face-first. I was just trying to go to the bathroom and tripped. You saved me from falling straight onto my stomach."

I was in as much shock that I caught her as she. We both knew it was Something much bigger than just my instincts that allowed me to wake up and catch her. God had answered my prayer from the weeks before and let me be her protector when she really needed it.

If God could work like this all the time, then maybe it would be easier to believe in Him. But that didn't matter for the time being. I was just glad He was there for that one brief moment when nothing else would have helped.

Mom's Mistake

There were days when I thought the world was crushing in on me. Keeping everything in has its side effects sometimes.

Trying to work all day in the sun and call Dee on my breaks to make sure she was ok, then coming home to see her in so much pain was hard for me to take a lot of times. There was one time in particular when Dee was in so much pain, she was just hunched over in a fetal position, with nothing she or I could do to relieve the pain. She had tried just lying in the tub with warm water for a few hours, on and off; I would bring her anything she asked for.

129

When I was at my limit of feeling helpless, the phone began to ring. Granny was on the other end, her concerned, tired voice breaking through the line.

"Hey, Timmie. I have some bad news to tell you." I paused and gave her the opportunity to continue. "Well, your mom had a spell. Those girls she watches during the day...well...she fed them rat poison."

"Rat poison?! And they ate it?"

"Yeah, I'm afraid so, and your stepdad as well. She put it in their macaroni and cheese."

"Well, are they ok? Where's Mom now?" I asked as my heart began to crumble. Like I even had to ask why.

"Well, the kids are still in the emergency room. They are pumping their stomachs now to release the poison. They took Mom into custody. If those kids' mom presses charges, she could go away for a long time." My body was giving up and I felt as if I was going to fall over.

"I have to go, Granny," I barely got out before being overcome with a cold heat, swelling with tears. I started pacing the kitchen, crying, and as I did, Dee opened the door from the bathroom and saw me in distress. Even though she was barely able to walk without being in pain and feeling nauseous, she came to my need, hugging and comforting me as I fell to the ground. In between sobs I told her what had happened and she just kept telling me how sorry she was every time, not even addressing her own pain anymore.

The weight of everything on my mind buried me. Consumed me. In a total state of shock, my body gave up and I feel asleep on the floor by the couch where Dee lay, holding my hand.

I was confused by how much this affected me. I had been craving for things to be normal between Mom and me ever since the day I found out that they weren't; it seemed that all the work in my mind was to no avail. I could never have that normal mom/son relationship with her always reminding me of my past—our past. The many nights I would wake up with her over our heads, contemplating stabbing us with knives or tin can lids. Or the times she would poison us, putting bleach in our milk or poison in our food. All the horrible parts of Mom that I tried to block out and hide from everyone now felt exposed, as what she had done would soon make local and even national news. I don't know what emotion haunted me more—sadness or anger or embarrassment.

This was one of the times I started questioning God again. Yeah sure, I was here for a reason...but can't You explain what that reason is already and stop making me suffer? This was the start of a new wave of stirred up emotions inside me, but for now I chose to suppress them again. I had gotten out a good cry and emptied some more space to store my hurt again for a while.

Time to keep rolling with the punches.

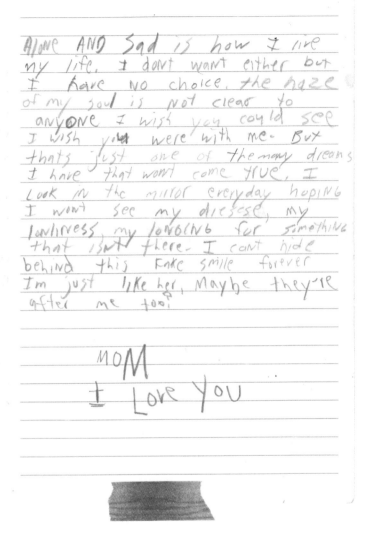

Alone AND Sad is how I live my life. I dont want either but I have no choice. the haze of my soul is not clear to anyone I wish you could see I wish you were with me. But thats just one of the many dreans I have that wont come true, I look in the mirror everyday hoping I wont see my diesese, my lonliness, my longing for something that isnt there. I cant hide behind this fake smile forever Im just like her, Maybe they're after me too.

MOM
I Love You

The Birth

To say Dee's pregnancy didn't go smoothly would be the understatement of the century.

Besides her being sick all the time, weak and just plain down-and-out, there were complications with the baby before he was even out of the first trimester. They saw things in the sonogram that showed signs that there might be some problems. Doctor visit after doctor visit, we found out that his feet were growing wrong too— club feet, which meant we already had an appointment set up for after he was born. Too stressed to be worrying about things like that, we tried to just take it day by day.

The months went by in a haze. A slow, sludgy, confused haze for both of us, with Dee having pain as a side effect.

On a Thursday, I got dropped off at my apartment for lunch, but fate had a different plan. Dee said, "I'm sorry to ask you this on your lunch break, but can you take me to the midwife's office? I think something is wrong." She didn't have to say anything more. I packed up her stuff, helped her into the car, and drove as quickly as I could to the office.

They nonchalantly checked her in and slowly took all her vitals, and hooked her up to a machine that drew squiggly lines on paper as a result of what's happening on the inside. When they finally got to her blood pressure and looked over her chart, the mood changed.

"How long have you been feeling like this?"

Dee answered grumpily, "Well, I told someone here about it two months ago and it's only gotten worse since."

The immediacy of the situation started to unfold as people were rushing around us, filling out paperwork, and making phone calls. "You need to get her over to the main hospital. We need to induce *now*!"

This came as a shock to both of us. I wasn't ready for this—she's not due for another few weeks. Underneath the speechless calm on my face, I was panicking. I drove the few blocks to the hospital where someone was waiting with a wheelchair for us to wheel her to a bed and get the process started. It was all so medical and foreign, like we were dreaming.

"Go get my main bag and Mama Kim please," Dee said with such a feeling of seriousness as they began inducing. I drove, crying because I couldn't figure out the mood of the hospital room—everyone was panicking like she was dying. Was she dying? Was our son dying? What was going on? These thoughts circled in my brain as I barely got the words out to Kim.

"Dee is in labor. She needs you."

She didn't hesitate; she had been through this enough times before to understand the seriousness and fear in my voice. She hugged me and told me to get back to the hospital. She would be right behind me.

True to her word, as soon as I got used to seeing Dee attached to so many tubes and machines, there came Kim, calmly walking in the door with a glow and peace wrapped all around her, transforming the tension in the room. She spoke to Dee, encouraged her that things were going to be ok and she wasn't going anywhere. She never once let on that she knew something wasn't right in the labor room, but instead covered those feelings in prayer and faith, trusting in something much bigger and unattainable that I couldn't quite grasp yet. I was still more than thankful for her being in the room.

Hours and hours went by. Dee's mom came in the room for a bit as well. I don't think she could stand to see her daughter in that much pain, because she had to leave a few times. I felt useless again, but I was good at something and that was letting Dee squeeze my arm as hard as she needed. Hours of agony, no epidural and teams of doctors and nurses all curious and concerned about her not rare condition: Preeclampsia + Toxemia + HELLP Syndrome.

Seventeen hours later, Kim was still there, speaking life into the room as Dee began to make her final pushes. I was at her head, letting her squeeze the life from my arm and Kim was coaching every breath she took until finally, he was out. The doctors laid him on a table a few feet from the foot of Dee's bed and immediately attached an oxygen mask as I took a picture, in shock at meeting our son for the first time. I supposed he was in shock too, it being his first time to see the world, because he was not making a single sound.

I only had time to snap a few shots before there was a team of doctors and nurses surrounding him, taking him to another room. Delirious and confused, Dee fell asleep in exhaustion a few moments after they took him away. She was too weak to hold him even if she would have had a chance.

I heard one of the nurses say he had an Apgar of one, not realizing the severity of that number until later. (Babies in good health, not requiring medical intervention, score eight to ten on their first Apgar test approximately one minute after birth.) He had come out struggling after the doctors had to use a force on him that we didn't approve of. He wasn't breathing on his own, so he had to lay in the baby ICU with a halo issuing oxygen to him. He was severely jaundiced as well, with extremely high bilirubin levels.

After Dee recovered a little bit, I wheeled her down to the ICU nursery so she could see her son—a tiny, beautiful creation enclosed in a plastic box with tubes and machines pumping into him. We looked past every tube and scary, unknown thing that was happening to him and just saw the love that was a perfect mixture of each of us—Odin.

The next day, we actually got to take him out and hold him, but only for a short time. They said they had done all they could for him at this facility; they would need more advanced tactics if they wanted to help him. I hated how they always spoke in code. We held each other as we signed papers and said goodbye to our son, only two days old, as he took his first flight to Dallas.

Her mom was right behind the helicopter to Dallas so our boy wouldn't be alone since Dee couldn't leave the hospital yet. That didn't last long. Refusing to stay hours away from him, the next morning Dee signed more papers agreeing that leaving the hospital was against medical advice in her condition. It was definitely one of the hardest nights and longest weekends we had ever had in our lives.

And this was just the beginning.

Dee stayed in Dallas all week with our son, calling and giving me updates on the phone. I wasn't allowed to leave work until Friday, so I was stuck in Tyler worrying until the next phone call. My boss's exact words:

"Are you a doctor? What good can you do, being at a hospital?"

My son was in critical condition a two-hour drive away and my boss was trying to justify his morals for not letting me off work. I was furious, but knew I had no control over the situation if I wanted to still have a job to support my fragile family. Friday could not come soon enough.

As I made my way to Dallas, it was the first time I had ever driven this far by myself—especially in a big city. I was scared, but I was even more determined to see my baby boy and beautiful wife.

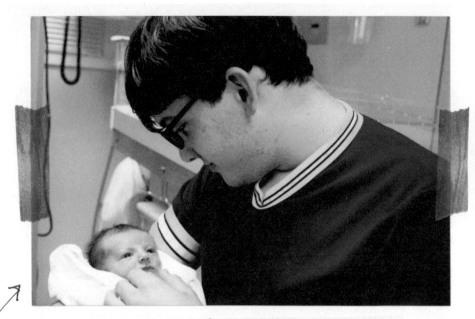

the first time i held him was
one of the first times i felt truly needed.

dee's mom is just as in love
as we are.

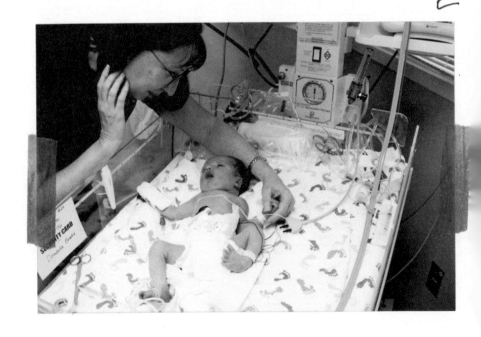

Getting to hold my son and change my first diaper ever, I was filled with confidence. The thing I had never had and knew nothing about, I now was...a father. I daydreamed about teaching him how to play guitar, taking him to shows, teaching him things a father never taught me how to do. I watched the nurses carefully, then would watch Dee, and mimic the same motions for burping, holding, changing and feeding.

I wanted to be the best father I could possibly be and Dee would become my biggest teacher. I learned by watching her and seeing her heart pour out in love over every action she did with our son. If I've done anything good as a father, I give her all the credit for being my muse.

After sleepless nights and more weeks away from my family, the day finally came. Dee and her mom were bringing our son home from the hospital to live at our house, in an actual crib surrounded by warmth as opposed to sterile white walls and tubes. It was the most welcoming sight I had ever seen walking through that door, his delicate round face asleep from the long ride. I took him from Dee's arms as we all lay resting in our own bed, enjoying each other as a family.

Too Many Doctors

Adjusting to life with a baby was one of the hardest transitions we ever had to make...especially with our son.

He couldn't sleep in a crib due to reflux that would cause him to projectile vomit if he was flat on his back (That was scary). He spent many nights asleep in a carseat lined with blankets beside our bed, or lying on my chest as I slept upright in a chair or on the couch.

We had more doctor visits than we had friend visits in the first few months, from going to Dallas to get exams and scans on his club foot to brain scans at a neurology clinic for kids. The brain scans only gave us more questions than answers. They also gave us the possibility that they might have to do a brain surgery—not another thing we needed to add to our plate, but we just wanted the best for our son. We didn't want to see him suffer.

All these tests and doctor visits soon became the norm.

I almost expected something else to happen. These days my faith was flip-flopping all over the place. A few days out of the week, I would be pursuing the truth of God, while the other half I was feeling sorry for myself, cursing God for putting such an innocent being like my son in so many horrible situations.

Since there were so many problems in the first few weeks of his life, one appointment we had put off was his circumcision. I went to the hospital with them, but for obvious reasons, opted out of being in the room while it was done. It was a very short procedure. They gave us some medicine to give him when we went home and number to call if we had any questions.

As we got home, I noticed his diaper had blood seeping through it. I freaked out and immediately called the on-call nurse. She told me that was normal—to change it and if it continued, give her a call back. I did as I was told, relieved a little bit that she didn't seem to be worried. As he was sitting on my lap about thirty minutes later, I felt a warm wetness on my leg—it was smeared with my son's blood, seeping through a second diaper. I changed him and got him ready to take to the emergency room as Dee was on the phone getting confirmation from the nurse that we needed to bring him in. We called Jessie and had her come with us.

Once we got there, we waited about forty-five minutes in the waiting room as another diaper filled with blood. They got him back and laid him on the table as Dee, her mom and I looked on in worry. Then a nurse came over and began taking samples of blood from him, one after the other.

"Should you really be doing that? Can't you see all the blood he has lost?"

"It just looks like a lot of blood, ma'am," she said with a know-it-all attitude. After the fourth vial of blood was sucked from his fragile body, all the color left him and he stopped breathing.

A panic rushed over the room as nurses and doctors scrambled around us. Dee was screaming and crying. My knees began to buckle and everything went white.

A few seconds later, I woke up on the floor of ER with a male nurse pulling me up, escorting me out of the room behind Dee and Jessie, all of us crying. A doctor had gotten through to Jessie first and told her he was stabilized now and recovering. She relayed the message to us and tried her best to make us feel like everything was ok, but we were broken. That one would take a while for my mind to recover from (if ever at all), but we had to put on our Mom and Dad faces again as he

The first hour of his life would change the whole course of ours...

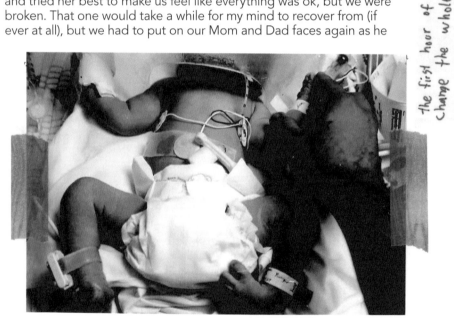

came out of surgery and we took him back to the safety of our home.

I tried my hardest to tell my son that I would never let anything like that happen to him again, but in all honesty; I knew I couldn't make that promise. It was one of the hardest emotions I had ever tried to come to terms with knowing that I wasn't completely in control of the things that could or could not happen to him.

I think it's a fear that comes with the territory, but I was determined to find a way to flush it.

An Angel

Maybe it was because he had so much to deal with in the first few weeks of his life... or perhaps a feeling of imbalance in the house due to whatever circumstances that were not seen by regular eyes. Whatever it was, Odin was upset.

All the time.

There were few breaks in the crying—at meal time and when he finally used every ounce of energy to cry himself to sleep. We took advantage of those times and slept for the small amount we could. It was definitely wearing us thin though.

I remember asking Boyd one day, tears filling up my eyes, "When will this end, the non-stop crying?" He reassured me, "The hard part only lasts until you get used to it."

these golden moments kept me going

Sometimes, Boyd talked in riddles and used cryptic wording, but for some reason, that was the most positive, clear statement I had heard in a long time.

Though I was slightly hopeful for the future, it didn't help the reality that was upon us. We learned a few little tricks, like letting him sleep in his carseat. If he laid flat, he would get sick, and there was the fear of him choking on it in the middle of the night. Sometimes we would put the carseat surrounded by pillows on top of the dryer as it spun to let him feel the vibrations and rhythms of the machine. When we did that we would back up chairs to the machines and maybe one of us would fall asleep. Us three with the laundry. He kept us up so much that eventually we had to take turns sleeping—two to four hours on and off, back and forth.

One night, I had missed my sleep and was fading quickly as Dee was having her rest. I was sitting on our purple velvet couch with the two books holding up the broken-off leg as Odin was screaming into my ear. I tried every hold and stand and cradle I could possibly think of. It was only getting worse. I sat down with him in my embrace, crying over my shoulder and did the only thing I had left.

I started crying too.

"God...help. I can't do this anymore."

As the tears streamed out, I felt a warm glow as if someone opened the door that was behind and to the right of me. The entire room lit up. Odin's eyes opened and his tears stopped. I could see a light gleaming off his eyes and could tell someone or something was behind me, but I could not turn around. It was like I was mortared to the couch like a brick wall. I saw a new expression on my son's face—a smile. A huge, heart-melting, genuine smile. The moment seemed to last for days, but in a matter of seconds, everything had passed.

I was crying loudly by this time, louder even than Odin. But they were tears of joy, knowing something other-worldly had just happened. Dee came out to see what was going on and all she saw was me crying, standing up now, looking back at the empty door with Odin in my arms, completely asleep.

"What's wrong? Is he ok...are you ok?" she asked frantically.

I replied under tears, "An angel just came in here."

She didn't ask questions, but started crying as well. She could hear the truth so thick in my voice she didn't need any questions answered.

All three of us lay in our room, Odin in his carseat beside our bed, and slept the most we ever had since he was born. God gave us the rest we needed to keep going.

Tests

Although we had gotten one night of respite out of weeks of ongoing crying and fits, it was short-lived. It seemed like he was crying even more now, so we were getting concerned. What now?

We knew he had a club foot so that was the first of the doctor appointments.

We drove to the Children's Hospital in Dallas where we met some of the greatest doctors of all time, with such amazing tact. They began Ponseti casting, which is where they gently take the club foot and turn it in intervals like a clock, then set it in a cast for a week. When we came back, they would break the cast off, turn it a little more and reset the cast, the purpose being that by the end of it, they over-corrected the turned foot. That way, when it would revert, it would revert into the natural position. This went on for a few months.

Finally, after multiple visits, the foot was where it was supposed to be. The next step was fitting him into special shoes with a bolted metal bar connecting them. With him having to wear these twelve hours a day that definitely didn't help his crying and frustration. These were some hard times—him wanting desperately to take off the shoes and us knowing his feet might not heal properly if we did.

Toward the middle of this process, we knew that, not only was he not developing in mobility, internally something was not right. All the milestones babies were supposed to reach, he had not. Now it was off to a different hospital for more tests. They thought maybe he had craniosynostosis, a birth defect that causes one or more sutures on a baby's head to close earlier than normal. Basically, it meant his brain was growing bigger than his skull had room for, is the way we were told.

Emotionally Dee and I were both drained. It was getting to a point where, if something bad possibly could happen, we expected it to. I tried my best to keep a good, positive attitude about these things but I'm sure it was a mostly-failed outward appearance. Inside I was broken, barely trying to hold on to the tiny bit of faith I had...and failing miserably. I could talk the talk, but no one would have been able to convince me of the truth. Life was, has been and will always be a struggle—with little "life vest" moments every now and then to keep me from drowning completely.

One night we found a little trick that would last for years. It was another of the bottom-of-the-bucket days; I had nothing left again and needed to be fished out. I was just sitting in front of our computer playing the lullaby cd to Odin as he cried and cried in my arms. Two o'clock in the morning and my shift with him had just started. I began praying as I did many times when I was desperate.

"God, I know this is probably punishment for the way I've led my life, but I need something, anything to help me get through this."

About ten minutes after I said that and no miraculous sign or angel this time, I got discouraged and just started flipping though iTunes. When I got to "Hey Jude", the first line from Paul's lips was like a silencer straight to Odin's mouth. His eyes widened and his mouth closed. The song lasted a little over seven minutes, and for the entire seven minutes Odin was quiet. The second the song went off, he started right up crying again.

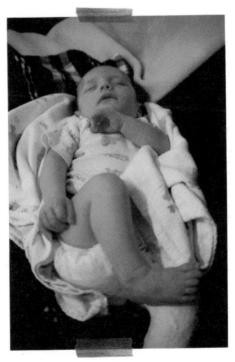

napping after being cast for his club foot

This has to be a coincidence—there's no way, I thought and played it again. The same magical spell was cast over my son. I started laughing, almost in disbelief at the situation, as I burned a disk of the song eleven times back to back and tried it from a CD player while he was in his room. It worked like a charm ninety percent of the time, every single night. God had yet again pulled through and helped us to find respite so we could deal with all the other difficulties.

After a few months of tests with drives to Dallas and its hospitals, they finally ruled out craniosynostosis and a few other brain problems, but still had not come up with a diagnosis. We would just have to wait for answers and see what, if anything, developed next.

House Hunting

June had come and almost a year had passed since Odin was born. We were feeling cramped. They don't tell you about all the stuff you gain when you have a kid—swings and dangling doo-dads and special eating chairs and changing tables. More room, please. We went to a realty company and decided to start the hunt for a more permanent living space.

The first place we looked at was nice...in that haunted, rundown, crooked house sort of way. We went in and looked around a few times; there was a loft upstairs that was super appealing. We thought someone might have been squatting up there because we would drive by sometimes and the light would be on. Other times it wasn't. We even went in once and as we were walking down, the door at the top of the stairs slammed shut and we ran screaming into the yard. We put an offer on it, but for whatever reason, it didn't go through.

The next few houses we looked at were ok, but either too small or too much money or someone would always come in and make a better offer. We were driving around the neighborhood and saw a "For Rent" sign on this amazing, cottage style, white brick house. We found an open door and walked in. It was a dream. Hardwood floors everywhere, a fireplace and mantle, a tiled bathroom. It was three bedrooms with a separate area that could be a dining room—I knew it would be perfect for my music room. There was a basement and a huge, fenced-in backyard.

This was our home, we just knew it.

The only problem was, it was not for sale and the rent was $300 more than we could afford. I called to see if the people would be interested in selling, and straight up, they said no. I don't think they even considered it. We left and thought about it for the week. We knew we had to be out of our apartment in two weeks or get sucked into another year lease there. I was just about to call the man who owned the house to tell him we were going to bite the bullet and rent, knowing it would be a stretch in our budget financially, when he called us instead. He asked if we were still interested in buying the house and without hesitation, we were all over it. Things were on the up again and within those two weeks we had a contract written, signed, sealed and delivered. We were now homeowners and it was time to move again.

With the help of our friends and their trailer, we made two huge trips and everything that was overcrowding our tiny little 700 square foot apartment now seemed to be merely scattered across the 1800 square feet we could call *home*.

CHAPTER NINE
Home

Adjusting

Having so much more room was such a nice change. We felt like we could actually have more than four people over without having to squeeze by each other like we were on a busy subway.

We moved in a bit before our son's first birthday. When he had his party we counted over 60 people there! It was so cool seeing how many people were in our house and all those people loved our son. Instead of "Happy Birthday" there was a special rendition of "Hey Jude" sung by every one of those harmonious voices. As time passed, holidays came and went and we would have the same size (or larger) gathering at each of them—Halloween dance parties, Friendsgiving, and awkward, dysfunctional family Christmases. It seemed the normal homeowner life. Of course we had our fill of tiny household disasters, from the toilet randomly spraying out from the back into the ceiling at two o'clock in the morning, to our ordeal of people stealing bikes and yard tools, but it was all good.

Meanwhile, Mom had been waiting in the county jail for her sentence to be enforced for the babysitting-poisoning-event. I didn't really know how to process this, but I made jokes to keep from being angry about it. I've never known how to process hurt feelings and maybe will never learn, but I am very tactful in knowing how to suppress these thoughts. So that's what I did. I decided to go with all my brothers to see her before she got shipped off to the state prison for who knew how long.

It was strange when we got there—all of my brothers, their kids and significant others, just waiting around in an old, stale, concrete waiting area. It had a cold, damp feel to it as if it was just a transition into what the actual jail cell felt like inside. Damp and cold and almost too quiet.

I got nervous. Being off drugs for all these years still hadn't cured my anxiety and fear of public figures, especially a building full of law enforcement. When we got to the tiny room, we had to take turns going in; as it began to come around to my turn, my palms got sweaty and I started getting a cold sweat like I was the one in trouble. The room was a small square with a built-in desk, a pull-out school chair and a black telephone on the wall. I sat down and almost didn't know what to say as I looked through an inch of glass at Mom's face, looking worn down in an orange jumpsuit. She smiled, I guess maybe to ease the tension...or maybe she didn't even notice it. I started making fun, laughing at her outfit.

"Where can I get one of those fancy suits?" I asked nervously.

"Well, I hope you don't ever have to wear one of these, " she answered back seriously, but with a slight chuckle.

"I'll never have to wear one of those. I'm the good one in the family now."

As I was laughing, she looked a little sad at herself and just said, "Yeah, I hope so." She asked if I was going to come visit her when they shipped her off, and I pacified her request, knowing I had no real intentions. Before we could say much else, the guard came in the door behind me and told us that time was up.

I told her bye, but I didn't tell her I loved her. I didn't want to feel as weak and vulnerable as she looked. This may be the last time I see Mom, I thought. I kinda didn't know how to react, but I felt my gut drop, and it was hard to cover up.

What did this mean? I hate wrestling with my thoughts.

Time to push them down inside...harder.

Answers

The stress of Mom being in a state prison compounded the stress of having a kid who still didn't have a diagnosis after more than a year struggling and searching.

We knew he was developmentally behind, so we found programs to try and help us. We had physical, speech and occupational therapists coming to the house once a week, but he was still making little to no progress. After another year and a half of tests, working diligently to get him to progress, we had only made minimal steps. The therapist cut-off was age three. He was rapidly approaching that so we looked into schools, but still had not come to terms that there was a "handicap" in our son. We kept thinking, "Oh, he will catch up. He doesn't need to be in a special school."

Finally, after touring a few regular ones, we got around to finding the St. Louis School. It was a school with the sole intent of helping special needs kids from ages three to twenty-one. While we were walking around, the warmth and love that poured out of every single worker, even down to the lunch lady, made us feel like this was the next step. We had a few tests to do with Odin before he was admitted, but these finally came up with some answers. He was finally diagnosed with low-functioning autism. Although it's not what any parent would be happy to hear, we were just excited that we finally had a reason he did certain things. Maybe we could learn how to let him be more comfortable in his environment.

After a week or so of enrolling, getting everything set in place, he started his first day of school. His teacher, Julie, was a definite Godsend. She glowed—you could feel how much she already loved our little boy the second we walked in the room. It was definitely hard leaving Odin with anyone that wasn't a part of his core babysitters, especially for the entire day. With Julie though, I had a confidence that he would be just fine.

As we were walking out the door, one of the management personnel from the school stopped us, wanting us to fill out forms to get Odin a wheelchair. In our heads, I know we were both thinking the same thing—why would Odin need a wheelchair? We just carry him wherever he needs to go. I think maybe it dawned on me, seeing so many of the other kids at the school in wheelchairs in the hallway, what the doctor had said to us before...that Odin probably would not ever be able to walk on his own without assistance.

It sunk in hard. I felt tears fill up my eyes and it was causing a chain reaction with Dee. Without hesitation, Julie came in to relieve the situation.

"No, don't worry about that right now. He is still little enough for us to get him where he needs to go. Just let us work on that. Don't think about that now." She gave a reassuring hug and told us that Odin was going to love it there. We both walked to the car and drove home without a word to one another. As Dee was at the house processing that information, I headed back to work, suppressing it with all the other hurts.

Walk the Line

It was the first Christmas break Odin had from school, and we were enjoying a little bit of rest from life in general.

The last few months had been full of trips to the hospital in Dallas to treat Odin's feet even more. They had given him AFOs which are basically leg braces that encase the entire leg up to a few inches above the knee and insert into a pair of shoes. They were made of plastic and strapped on with blue velcro to match the Superman decal on the back of them. Needless to say, Odin hated wearing these, as well as the standing table device that he used at home and school to strengthen his leg muscles and motivate him to walk.

The feeling of helplessness you have as a parent, watching your child scream and not knowing if it's in pain or he's just pissed off at you for making him do things that may or may not be out of his ability...it's sickening to a point. If this worked it could change his quality of life. If it didn't, he could just hate me forever and never be able to tell me. That's the way I felt about it, but I just kept trying.

One afternoon during the holiday, we put the braces on him. As we watched him hold on to a door, we saw him standing for the longest we had seen yet. We rewarded him, and afterwards just let him lay in his bed and rest. The braces were kind of a pain to get on and off, so we left them on for the time being and went to the front room to watch a movie. About halfway into it, we heard a commotion in the kitchen.

What we saw would rock our world forever.

It was our two-and-a-half foot 3 year old, scrambling, his arms flailing from side to side, grinning from ear to ear...walking for the first time. From his bedroom all the way into the front entertainment room, he walked. Tears filled both DeAnda and my eyes and laughter the likes of which our house had never heard poured out. After all the doctors had said and how much it seemed like the world was out to get him, our son defied it all and made his own rules.

The ironic part of the day was that we had been watching the movie *Walk The Line*... and that he did.

From then on, our son was mobile, getting more and more balanced as he walked. Sometimes he would get me in trouble. Because he was still a little bit wobbly, I would have a protective barrier of my long, gangly arms reaching out from behind him on either side so he would have a bar to catch himself on if he started to lose balance. One of his favorite places to run free was the coffee shop where Dee worked. While we waited for her to go on break, we would spend an hour walking from one side of the store to the other.

This place was particularly busy one day, and as Odin was walking past the bar, he kind of slipped up on his shoe and fell hands-first into the first thing in front of him—a young girl, maybe eighteen or nineteen. His hands dug right into the back of her skirt as he regained balance and started back on his run to the other side of the store. When the girl looked down in furious anger, all she saw were my hands held out in the safety net formation, but no Odin. No time to react or tell her what had happened—Odin had seen an open door and was headed straight to it. I just had to accept the evil hatred this girl had for what she thought I had done.

even with leg braces, he finds a way to get out of all situations

This would not be the last time Odin ever used his twisted sense of humor to humiliate me, but I wouldn't change it for the world.

Luvbeat

It's funny how things you never think you would do end up finding a way into your life. Say a hip-hop band...never in my life had I ever had a desire to do something even remotely similar.

Three of the DuPree sisters had started a band a several years back with their oldest brother, Weston, on the drums. They had just signed to a major label and this entailed a lot more time away for him...and a lot more trying to figure out how to make that time pass quickly for his girlfriend, Jessie Rae. She was one of our best friends and since pretty much the entire family was in the band, we were all sad—missing our friends and family. I had the brainiac idea of starting an old school R&B group/Destiny's Child-type thing as a distraction. I could make the music—Dee, Jessie Rae and Christie DuPree could be the vocalists.

I wrote the first beat and melody with a little bit of lyrics. We spent the day recording, being total idiots and having a blast. When it came time for Christie to record her part, she wasn't really feeling it. She had gotten sick the night before, so in the spot where her vocals were supposed to go, I decided to write a rap and do it myself to be funny. The girls actually really liked it and said the song was complete. We showed it off to our first audience—Mama Kim, in the front room of her house. She was so enthusiastic about it I almost thought she was kidding. She reassured us she wasn't, telling us we had to get more songs and even do a live gig. We all laughed at the idea, but knew deep down that we had something special between us.

Over the next few weeks we began writing more and more, recording another song we thought even better than our first. When Weston came home, the band said we had to open for them at a local show they were doing. We reluctantly agreed; it was the most nerve-wracking thing I had ever done. The girls were used

we got bling-bling

we got cd's

we got merch

145

to it due to theater arts classes, but I was at a point where I thought I might puke or pass out. We made up synchronized dance moves to make it even more ridiculous, and in the first ten seconds, I saw the crowd trying to kinda figure out what was happening.

By the end, we had won them over. They were screaming for an encore, but we didn't have any more songs. The thrill of that day was felt between all three of us, and we knew it was something we needed to pursue.

Within a few months, a good friend from Dallas, Daniel Hall, helped make us known in the recording studio where he worked. During a break from recording, he played our demos though the house speakers so the producer could hear. To my surprise, the producer was actually interested enough that he got my number and called me the next day. I explained that we barely had the money to buy gas to get to Dallas, let alone pay to have something professionally recorded when we got there. He told me that he did a free project of albums he truly believed in once every year. This year, that was us. I was blown away by the generosity and sincerity of his heart—a true genius of the arts.

Over the next few weeks and months, we would take weekend trips to Dallas to record more when we could and when it fit into his schedule. We were playing more and more shows now, growing a fan base and gaining more popularity. The dream that we could do this and make profit from it was starting to become a reality inside my head.

Finally, a year after we started recording, our album was finished. What to do next with this skillfully sculpted work was up in the air.

A New Business

After years of being pushed around, working for others and not making nearly what I felt I was worth, I knew it was time for a change. The only thing was, I didn't feel I was good at anything else and didn't have the confidence to start my own business. So I just switched companies to see if that would help.

For a while it did. I was treated better, got paid a little more, and if I needed extra, there was extra work to do. It all seemed to be going well until the boss decided to sell the business to a rich kid and his dad who knew nothing about window cleaning. That's when the workload started to double, doing both our route and seventy-five percent of the new owners' work too. This was without getting paid more, just working harder and longer hours. I don't think most people in the world completely love what they do for work. That's why it's called work—not "hey, let's get paid to do what we want." But I think that, with the extra stress of home life, I was just bitter, irritable and not myself—or at least who I would want to be. It would come out in daily conversations with Dee and friends.

Finally, a friend started asking me questions about it one day. How much would it cost to start up my own business? What all would I need? He saw the answer, clear as day, and invited me over for a meeting.

"You order whatever ladders and tools you need. I will give you my credit card number and let you buy it. Be looking for a truck and call me the minute you find an affordable one that runs well; I will wire you the money. Let's start being business partners."

I was in shock. Was this really going to happen? Could I be self-sufficient?

We worked out the details. For the first year, I would keep any money I made. Starting in January, I would pay $100 a month until the bill had been paid off. After that, we would work out a percentage he would get from any profits I made. Everything seemed reasonable and fair, so we got started. I ordered the ladders and all my equipment and laid it in the front living room of our house while I searched for a truck.

It wasn't a week later that I found the perfect one in the Walmart parking lot—a 1996 extended cab, gold Ford Ranger. The price on the window said $2,500 and had a number. When I called and offered $2,200, the lady said she could meet me there in two hours with the key.

After I called my friend, I went into Walmart where, like he promised, he had wired me the money. I paid for my truck and now had the key. One problem—this truck was a standard. I didn't know how to drive a stick shift and my best friend who did, didn't have his license. We called his dad and he was there within twenty minutes, taking my prize home.

For the next few weeks I practiced and practiced—stalling on hills, rolling backwards at lights and peeling out, leaving trails as I drove. I finally got the hang of it and was able to start soliciting clients and doing real work. It was strange how easily this came for me. Maybe being a face washing windows in the area for so long gave me the advantage, or maybe it is the southern-charm voice I subconsciously go into when bidding a client. It's like I can't even stop myself. When I hear my voice, I'm thinking...who am I?

Whatever it is, it's working and being my own boss has been one of the best solutions I've found to loving your work. And I have something that's mine (or at least partly mine) that I'm proud of.

Deal Or No Deal

A few years into building my own window cleaning company, I think it started to wear on me.

I had only built my company high enough so that it wouldn't interfere with what I thought was going to be my cash boat—my music. We were playing more and more shows, getting bigger recognition from people that mattered. With the help of friends who were already on labels, the word was getting out. It was always a secret obsession of mine to get huge with this band, and I knew it was a very conceivable possibility.

I think I just wanted a break. A break from the stress of a kid who, at five years old, would still cry constantly for reasons we never knew. He would bang his head against chairs, floors, walls, strollers—all just to inflict enough pain for him to start crying. It was mind weights in my head all the time.

I wanted a break from working in the freezing cold and the extreme Texas heat.

I just wanted to not have to worry about money and finances so much.

The ironic thing was that I liked the fact that we were not on a label, doing everything DIY. A few labels even asked us to sign, and though my heart was jumping at the idea, I had built up a barrier against giving in to the industry's wants. I liked people wanting us and getting to say no—a very intense tug-of-war in my mind.

Plus, I knew that all three of us didn't want the same thing as a whole. I knew at times that Dee and I had visions of signing and getting paid to do this, but then we had the burden of what to do with Odin. I never felt that Jessie Rae wanted it as much as we did. I think her thing was that she was already away from her love enough with him being on tour with his band. If she started doing the same thing, it would have just made it that much more difficult.

For now we just came to the agreement of playing gigs whenever friends would ask us to open or for special events, but other than that, we would never do it for full-time work.

And that was that.

Really Bad Vacation

A series of unfortunate events—this seemed to be the anthem for my life.

Dee had some time off and knew we needed a family getaway to just reconnect. We planned a week in the summer to go visit her sister in Corpus Christi. The week before, I started getting things ready.

The A/C in our car had gone out, so I ordered a part online and got my mechanically smart brother to come help me install a new fan for it. One hundred bucks out of our budget, even though he refused to take the full amount I tried to give him. Then on to the next task.

Our inspection was out and I knew that we would need to have that taken care of for that long of a trip. They asked for my insurance card; I couldn't find a current one. I called our insurance rep, and he informed me that we hadn't paid for it to be covered and were two months behind. In order for us to have it reinstated, we would need to pay the two months, plus six more in advance. That would have cut into the majority of what we had to spend on vacation, so I decided to just call a different agent with cheap rates that I had heard about on a TV commercial.

I find the address and am heading that way when I see it flash past me on the left out of the corner of my eye. I think, if I turn right, I can just loop around and then hit the parking lot. While I was sitting at the red light, a motorcycle cop turns left in front of me, then immediately pulls a u-turn with his lights flashing on me. I continue my turn and park in the lot of the insurance agency. When I tell the cop what I was doing and give him the whole story, fighting tears, he just says, "Oh wow...I guess today just isn't your day. No inspection is bad, but insurance is a no-no." And hands me a ticket.

Even the insurance agency thought it was the worst thing he could've done. I finally got my insurance and inspection, $450 later. I had this thought of how disappointed Dee would be in me for not having our car covered, so I just never told her—one of the many financial problems I would keep from her.

A few days before we left, I was dealing with the ticket; I even had to go to court to talk to a judge. He put me on a payment plan so I wouldn't have to pay it all at once. Luckily for me, not only did I get to pay $350 for the initial ticket, but for the next three years I would have to pay out $300 per year on a payment plan as well. What started as a small problem ended up costing me huge. I planned to sweep it all under the rug and enjoy my vacation.

We knew it would be too heavy of a trip on Odin to drive the complete seven and a half hours straight, so we broke up the trip. After three or four hours we were in Houston at Dee's uncle's house—already tired, hungry, exhausted needing rest to make it the rest of the way to our final destination. Odin decided he hates it in Houston and started screaming and kicking. We would calm him down and right when we thought he would fall asleep, he would start crying and kicking again. We tried different rooms, beds, couches, floors, cars...nothing would help. This went on from about 9 pm at night until 7:30 am when everyone in the house finally woke up. I think I maybe got a twenty minute nap, on and off.

Dee said, "If you take him and feed him, let me have just a two hour nap, I can finish the trip driving." So that was the plan. As soon as we started driving again, Odin closed his eyes and was out like a lamb for the rest of the journey. I think both of us were slightly regretting our vacation so far, and maybe me more so, knowing what had transpired just a few days earlier.

Once we got to Corpus Christi we were greeted warmly to an amazing Spanish house with a huge swimming pool in the backyard, just literally blocks from the ocean. It was a much-needed break in the tone of the atmosphere and for the next few days, we started to have fun.

One the fifth day, we decided to go to a museum downtown by the beach. I was driving and singing, making up my own words to the music we had blasting to keep Odin happy. As we went through a stoplight, I saw the building. I put my signal on and turned left. What I didn't see was a whole other lane with a huge, new, red pickup just behind me.

It T-boned us so hard in the driver's side back door that it popped two of our tires and spun us a good 180 degrees. The smell of burned rubber and salty gravel, sand and smoke was blended together in a way that only an "after wreck" smell has. Dee was screaming and crying for Odin—I was just crying in shock. Odin had a toy in hand, just sitting still and smiling. As soon as Dee opened the door, he started laughing like it was the greatest thing I could've done.

The thought that I put my son and wife in danger was one of the most heart-wrenching feelings I had ever known. It was my fault. It was heavy and it stuck with me.

After we got out and accessed the situation, all of us were ok, including the lady driving the truck. The same could not be said about our car—it was totaled. Looking on in total confusion, I then got another ticket for improper lane crossing. Just a little icing for the topper.

When we got picked up by our brother-in-law, to our surprise, we saw Dee's dad. He had been in town for a vacation too and was leaving to go back home the next day to beat a tropical storm that was coming. So there was one good thing...at least we had a way home. That is, if we didn't die in the process.

About twenty minutes into the trip, the rain was coming down so hard it was just sheets of water covering the windows, but that didn't stop Dee's dad from going ten to fifteen miles over the speed limit the entire way. We must have hydroplaned a good twenty-five times, each one taking my stomach away from us. I just knew Dee was gonna lose it before we made it home.

After seven and a half hours of driving hell, with little or no stops, we reached home. Miserably hot and exhausted, we drug ourselves into the equally hot house, cranked the A/C and just lay there, falling asleep in exhaustion. The funk was so thick that even the air we breathed was heavy with it.

This would be known as "The Worst Vacation Ever".

The Miracle

Over the next few months, I would delve into some of the darkest moments of my life.

Having this dream of one day magically being signed and making loads of money had taken a toll on me. It had taken a toll on the entire family, except they were not

this didn't seem to faze him at all.

even aware of the totality of it. I had been neglecting important things like work and bills and the pressure was starting to build. It started with me letting one month pass by without paying our mortgage—I just knew by the time it was due again, we would be rich enough to pay both payments. This fantasy blocked my perspective of reality to the point where we continued to live like we had enough money to do the simple things in life, like eat and go to movies and buy clothes.

Each time the first of the month would come, and we still would not have that extra few thousand in the bank like I thought we would, the pressure would build higher and higher. The idea of being the only one who knew about this was also an added level. I didn't tell Dee or any of my friends about my struggles. I just waited, month after month, for them to go away on their own. I had gotten to the point where I wouldn't even let the mail be seen for fear there would be a late notice on our house. I kept the other bills paid, the more noticeable ones. I figured Dee might start asking questions if we didn't have water or electricity one day.

In February I got a notice in the mail saying there would be an auction for our house on March third at 10:30 am.

I called to try to get an extension on the date so I could come up with some mastermind plan to pay the debt we owed, but to no avail. I had let ten months slip past without making a mortgage payment. I've always been a last second kind of guy, but this was taking it to the most intense extreme possible. If I didn't come up with $9,000 by March third, our house and all of our security would be gone.

On March second, I finally broke down and told my friend Sam what was going on. I told him everything and was just crying while he sat there in silence. After a moment, he spoke.

"There's only one thing to do—pray for a miracle." He paused again. "You need to tell DeAnda. Right now. God will not do anything until you break down and tell her the truth."

I wanted to do anything other than that, but I knew in my heart it had to happen. With the most fear I had ever faced in my life, I walked back to my house and told Dee I needed to tell her about something really stupid I had done. She could see the seriousness dripping off my face in the form of fear and tears. I told her every detail of how I had betrayed her trust and of our financial situation...that we had to have $9,000 by 10 am the next morning or we wouldn't have a place to live...and about how we had $50 in our account at the moment.

Her jaw dropped at every sentence I spoke, as if I were a boxer, delivering blow after blow. Her response was what you might have expected. If earthquakes, typhoons, tornados and the power of ocean waves all formed together and got stuck inside a person in physical form, that's what each word and gesture coming from her body would have looked and felt like. The most rightful answer for being so wronged.

"Nine thousand dollars? How could we ever come up with that in one day?!" She finally left the room in pure disgust from looking at me. And I crumbled. I knew I had to at least try and figure something out, so I lifted myself up and walked back over to Sam's apartment.

I started crying out to God, begging for help. As I lay there, Sam said his band would do anything they could. An hour later, after checking the band budget, their manager came over with $3,000 in an envelope for me. I was in shock.

I kept getting bombarded with calls of people who loved us, asking what was going on and how they could help.

My friend Adam told me to meet him in the Starbucks parking lot. When I got there, he hugged me, stuck another envelope in my back pocket and said, "It was all my bank would allow me to withdraw for a day. I hope it helps! I love you."

As soon as he drove off, Jessie Rae and Weston were in the same parking lot with yet another envelope containing $1,600 in it.

In a matter of a few hours, I had $7,600. How was this happening?

I drove back to Sam's with the money I had accumulated, only to find a slew of friends I knew and even some that I didn't, each handing me folds of hundreds and sticking different bills in my pocket as I cried and hugged them all.

At 8 pm I was $300 shy of having the entire sum.

Our producer called me. He said, "Is it true...what I've been hearing? Be honest with me."

I told him everything about how much I had screwed up and he reassured me that everyone screws up. Though I don't know how confident I was about it at the time, he told me that Dee would eventually heal from this and not leave me. He told me to check my Paypal account—he had put $500 in there.

"Use the extra to buy groceries for the house you will be raising your children in."

I sat praying, thanking God for being so fruitful when I barely even believed in Him. If anything was a wake up for my faith, it was this moment. I crawled back to my house to find DeAnda sitting on the couch, obviously completely distraught. Her only words to me—"So...now what?"

"I...I got all the money. Well, God got it for me..." She wasn't about to praise me for making our friends feel sorry for us and lending us money. I explained that no one wanted money back—it was all gifted. I had told every single person that she didn't have anything whatsoever to do with the situation we were in. It was completely my screw-up.

She was still so hurt and just said she couldn't be around me yet. I understood and slept on the couch that night...and for the next few months. Healing takes time and I would just have to wait and truly seek God for myself, not just let Him be my life vest for the idiotic situations I get myself into.

In the morning I went to the bank to transfer the money to our mortgage company and save our house from foreclosure—a completely unnecessary close call. The pattern of bottling up feelings and information had been cracked, but wasn't even close to being broken yet.

Write It Down

As the next few years passed, things would eventually seem to be in order, at least on the outside.

My business picked up again; we were not behind on a single mortgage payment or on any other bill. I was allowed to sleep in my own bed again, and Dee was regaining her trust in me little by little. We even took our first international vacation to Rome, Italy. There we learned to depend on each other even more since only ten percent of the people we were around spoke English. Things appeared to be going better than ever...and that's how it usually is when secretly, things are the worst on the inside.

I had twenty-five years of deeply suppressed emotions crammed inside me like an overstuffed toy animal. Instead of a soft, cottony feeling, it was like being filled with tar—sludge-black and putrid. I began to lose not only the little faith that I had, but I started to even despise God. At moments, I think I even hated Him and the whole idea of Christianity.

I was having a lot of thoughts about my past, wondering why, if God was so merciful, did I have to be put in certain situations all my life. Any time I would hear something on TV or in a movie that brought even a passing mention of molestation or child mistreatment, I would feel an intensity come over me. I needed to act normal—I felt like everyone would know the things I didn't want them to know about me, things that I had never even told my own wife. Things Mom may not have even known. Things I would never tell my brothers in a million years. Hurtful, disgusting things that I felt so ashamed of it drove me past being sad...to just being furious. And that's when I would take it out on God, to hide the fact I was so hurt from everyone that knew me as the happy, always cheery guy.

On many occasions I would get in fights with Dee, and the stem of what started anything was the hurt I was avoiding. When I'm upset subconsciously, I want everyone to feel just as bad as I do, so I then purposely act like a brat. I'm really good at it. I could probably put the Dalai Lama in a bad mood. One particular day, my wall finally crumbled and my insides were exposed.

I had been working all day. When I came home, Jessie was visiting Dee, and they were making sandwiches. I hadn't gotten much sleep the night before, or really the entire last couple of weeks. I would have nightmares about what Mr. Coffee did to me when I was younger—one of the darkest secrets I had kept from even DeAnda. It was making me so angry I couldn't even think straight. Dee, as sweet as she always is, asked if I wanted a ham or turkey sandwich.

"Turkey," I told her and sat down, just listening to her and Jessie's conversation on and off, trying to fake a happy mood.

After a few minutes, I came out of a daydream to see a smiling face and a ham sandwich on my plate. The smile quickly faded and the only thing I saw was this HAM sandwich.

Ham? She made me ham? Didn't I just say I wanted turkey? She's just doing this to piss me off. She's tired of me and wants to make me so mad that I leave her. I bet she and Jessie were talking about this before I got here. What can I do to get him out of my life?

My mind thought through the entire situation so irrationally, but so thoroughly that it became real to me. I spoke up.

"I'm not eating this!! You made this sandwich out of hatred!!" And I stormed off, grabbing my keys, slamming the door, peeling out and driving away, not even giving Dee or Jessie a chance to get in a word. They began frantically calling my phone and leaving messages, but I didn't pay it any mind. Tears were flowing as the irrational thoughts started up again.

If she wants me to leave then fine—let's just see what she does without me. I'm not ever going back. I don't need to be around someone who doesn't want me. Forget it!!

Then I went into a daydream as I drove, every hurtful event in my life coming into plain view. I started crying even harder—it got to the point where there were so many tears I had to pull over. By this time I was all the way out to the State Park, about ten miles from our house. As I looked around with red, puffy eyes and tear-stained cheeks, trying to figure out where I was and how I even got there, I heard a voice.

"That'll be five dollars, please. Sir? It's five dollars to go in here..." It was the park ranger trying to collect money.

I just stuttered, "Oh, I'm sor...sorry, I was just trying to get to...to...the highway."
It was the only comprehensible sentence I could manage to slur out of my mouth.

"Oh...I-20? Yeah, you just passed it—turn right around here and you can't miss it."

I clumsily thanked her and started my drive back, this time a much more sobering drive. I knew if I didn't get help, real help, I would lose my mind. It runs in the family, and I was getting close to that gene. Quickly.

It had been around thirty minutes at this point. When I got home, Dee was on the porch with her phone. She wasn't mad like I expected her to be. She took me in her arms and asked me to talk. I told her I was just so mad, all the time. I told her about my hurts as a child. I admitted that I use humor to cover up my pain, and I always had. I admitted that I needed help...and that was the hardest part for me. I'm so independent, and I always think I can figure out and manage on my own, but it's not true. Everyone needs help with something at some point in their life—sometimes on a way larger scale, sometimes just with something as small as listening. The one thing I didn't tell her was how much I was starting to really despise Christianity.

Baby steps, I thought—can't completely overwhelm her.

She gave me two suggestions; one I accepted and the other I stubbornly ignored. She said I needed counseling sessions, and I needed to write down the hurts and past memories that were hard for me to deal with.

When I went to my counselor, he asked me the most ironic question in my first session.

"Have you ever tried writing the things you can't voice to get them off your mind?"

Really? Good thing these things are confidential. Dee doesn't have to know he said it too, I thought.

Eventually I gave in and let my fingers vomit out the hurts of my life into document after document on my computer. After a few months, I had a few years worth of childhood hurts typed out. I let Dee read the very first entry. Tears filled her eyes.

"Tim, what the heck? This is actually good. You're a writer!"

" 'Actually good'—wow, is that a compliment?" I said jokingly.

"No, seriously though...with your education, or lack thereof, it's really surprising. Babe, I think you're supposed to write a book."

With that, I kind of chuckled, knowing there was absolutely no way in the world I could ever write a book. Over the next few weeks she kept bringing it up, encouraging me, even letting a few of our friends read it. Then, they started encouraging me to keep it up. From then on, I decided that I would keep trying.

If I ended up failing...well, at least I tried.

The Final Truth

Over the next few years I would continue my process of journaling, writing down memories, reliving the past and maybe try to learn something from it.

That I did indeed.

I was angry. As much as I wanted to say I was over it, I have to admit the truth—I was far from that. Ninety percent of my friends at the time were Christian believers and that's all great and everything, but your church is cheesy. This invisible entity that controls every aspect of your life and judges you if you're bad and rewards you with an awesome life if you're obedient? I'm not buyin' it. But I will pretend to.

If I said what I was thinking, it would cause an atomic eruption in my marriage and in my social life. I was known for being this happy-go-lucky guy that believed in God and was your semi-typical American dad to some degree. All on the outside.

Inside I was thinking...is there really something greater?

I mean, I've seen the power of darkness—was that just coincidentally scary? Were they just visions I had from so many drugs before and after I was born?

Were the things I prayed to God about that came true...were they just a coincidence and my life was just lucky for little increments in between the heartache and pain?

Then I wondered, If He is real...Why did God let all these things happen to me? If He has control over everything, couldn't He have left out the sucky parts?

I struggled internally with this pretty much most of my life. Then as I grew older, I just became more and more cynical. I couldn't even hear a worship song without thinking how ridiculous it sounded. Through all of these thoughts, I had to maintain the personae of being "Christian" in front of friends and family, so I went about normal life just being goofy, crazy Tim that everyone loved. I was an adult now, and had to take care of my family and be responsible. I didn't have time to wrestle that spiritual stuff.

As I was very aware of bills (especially our mortgage) now, I had everything worked out perfectly in my head each month, paying and taking care of bills, until one day I came across a snag. I got a letter saying they were raising my mortgage payment by almost four hundred dollars. I called the bank immediately and asked how I could change this payment back to the amount it had been; they went through a slew of options that I didn't fully understand. The one I chose was a re-modification, and knowing the pain that I had caused in the past, knew I needed to do whatever I could to make sure that didn't happen again.

They sent me paperwork a mile high to fill out, mark Ts and cross Xs. I did and sent it back. They told me the re-modification could take six to twelve weeks and not to worry about making a payment until it all went through. As my brain was so busy with other things, I never even said anything about it to Dee, not trying to keep anything from her; it just wasn't on my radar that I even needed to tell her.

After almost three months of calling to make sure everything went through, I was told we were just in a waiting process and not to worry—I would not be penalized for the payments that I was not paying. With that peace of mind, I kind of forgot about it and was just waiting until the fourth month when I got a letter saying that I would have to re-submit my re-modification papers because it was lacking one sheet of paper. So I did and the three-month waiting process started again.

Just another waiting game. No big deal.

Things were going really well, and even though my mind was still struggling with unbelief, I was happy...on the surface anyway. I even tricked myself into thinking I truly was happy.

My friend Danny called me up and told me his genius idea for a book + soundtrack creation he'd had in the works for years. He finally wanted to get an official start on it, and invited me to California to start the writing process of music making. I jumped on the idea, not even fully aware of what I was getting myself involved with. Dee was so happy for me; I packed my little suitcase and within a few weeks, I was on my way to start my new endeavor.

As I was getting off the plane and in the car to start my week long vacation/work trip, I got a call from DeAnda. She sounded somber and serious, asking if I could talk. Now.

I knew something was serious, but had no clue what it was about. I thought maybe something had happened to Odin by the seriousness of her tone of voice. She told me she got a note on our door telling us to call the mortgage company. She did, and they told her we were six months behind on our mortgage and our house was in a state of foreclosure—again.

It was news to me as I tried to explain to her what I did, not realizing how big a deal re-modifying a loan was. I really thought I was doing us a favor. The mortgage company had said nothing to me about our house being in foreclosure; I thought it was just a natural process. She sounded disappointed and upset at me, but she didn't sound angry. She was speaking rationally but sternly, letting me know the weight of what I had done.

I got off the short conversation with her and called my mortgage company as Danny and his mom drove me back to their house where I would be staying. They told me our house was in a state of foreclosure only because, when you don't pay mortgage for over four months, legally they have to put your title in that folder. They had sent out a notice because they thought a paper was missing from the re-modification papers I had faxed in, but they found it after the notice had been sent to the house.

Even though I was told not to worry, I should have at least explained that to DeAnda, but my brain doesn't think in the rational way of the world most of the time. The process was still underway and we were still in a waiting process, but now Dee knew about it. And I realized I had screwed up again—not in the same way or magnitude as last time, but in the fact that I should have been honest with Dee and just told her about the re-modification.

I called Dee back as I walked around the front yard of Danny's house. He and his mom carried my suitcase inside and waited for me. Dee started speaking truth into me as I apologized, knowing I had hurt her again, the diamond-eyed girl that I loved more than anything in the world. She told me she had felt a distance from me for months and couldn't quite pinpoint it—we were like two ships passing in the night. She said I felt empty and sad and she was praying for me. I tried to deny it; she reassured me that she knows me way better than I think she does. She told me that I needed to seek the Lord and truly find myself. She was glad we had the week apart so she could reassess things and so I could learn without her. She got off the phone and her tone was so heartbreaking.

I knew in that instant, I was either going to break or figure myself out. I stood looking to the sky, speaking aloud.

"God, if You're there, if You're real, if You want to use me, You need to show me! I don't want to be a constant failure anymore, but You are so hard to believe in!" Then I screamed profanities at the sky, to the Creator.

It brought me to my knees—the honesty and true fear I felt for calling out the Figure I had been struggling with believing in. In that moment, it felt like a wave of warm honey swept my entire body. With everything I could muster I spat out my doubts one after the other "Where were you when I was hurting? Where were you when no one else wanted me?!" I heard almost audibly a voice saying, "Give me all your doubts." And so I did. I went through every moment I could think of where I felt unloved and asked where this "father" figure that everyone talked about was. Wave after wave of hurts were being thrown into the sky. With each word I said, it felt like I would sink further until my face was cheek to cheek with the freshly-cut, sweet green grass. I was laid out completely and every time I tried to get up, another wisp of the truth would sweep over me, almost telling me, "I'm not through with you—stay down!" I spent at least thirty minutes crying, going through my hurts. I kept hearing in my mind, "Let it out. These are not yours. They belong to Me—I am the Father you've been seeking." The only emotion or sound I could get out of my mouth after that was crying—no, sobbing. Body shaking, convulsing, chest-heaving, snot bawling.

In that moment, I felt it.

Truth. Pure and simple. Like when a mother scoops up her crying baby melting on the floor and soothes him to sleep. I was being cradled by my Godly father. He was reiterating all the times he was there and showing me moment by moment where he was.

In that instant, my cynicism washed away with the river of tears coming down my face. As I went through all of the thoughts, I knew without a doubt God had saved me and was going to use me + my hurts for others to experience the same truth I was. I didn't know how yet, but still...it didn't matter. This moment would change the way I see things for the rest of my life. I know it wasn't just an experience I had, but an encounter. A true, life-changing encounter.

In the middle of my brokenness on the front lawn, I saw Danny's dad walk past me. He obviously knew something big was happening, but he coolly walked inside, not interrupting my scene. They all waited for me around the table without touching mom's carefully prepared dinner until I had come inside. I finally gathered the strength to walk back in. After I explained, they prayed over me, one after the other, for at least an hour. Then we shared a meal. I rested most of that first day and then each day after I tried to learn more about this Creator, while working on myself the rest of my time in Cali.

Starting this music project with Danny would be a very critical, even a very God-timed, moment in my life. I came home, the beginning of being a changed man.

Dee and I worked through things over the next few months, growing together as a team rather than playing two separate pieces in a game. Our marriage was growing, spiritually and mentally, learning from each other how to better communicate.

It took another six months of waiting for our mortgage to finally work itself out, but once we got that hurdle under our belts, I think the most healing and growth started to take place. We began worshipping together with music and were for the first time really spiritually connected as a family.

Being made new ten years in...It was an amazing feeling.

this family held me together

my california family

EPILOGUE

The last pages! I figured I would give you fair warning. It's like when you are eating a bag of chips and you eat the last one thinking there's more in the bag...so disappointing.

***

No matter your story, it's kind of funny and surreal looking back on the most memorable parts of your life and reliving them. Memories are funny that way. Some stories I thought I would never let out. I wanted to keep them caged, pushed down so deep that the memory would just decay and eventually rot out, but I found that in the release there is a relief that no words can explain. I've cried and poured myself out whole, vulnerable, as the vivid moments drip from my thoughts into words on a page breaking light from the darkest moments of my life. These dripped out moments became a story—a story that was never meant for anyone's eyes but mine. This was all just a journaling process to cope with things my voice never had courage enough to even mumble. In the process I have learned to heal and grow from wrongs that have been done to me and mistakes that I have made. I have learned to manage and begin to heal from a pain so thick that I thought the weight of it would eventually break me.

My Process

Since I have started voicing parts of my story and my past, I am often asked questions like: *"How is it possible you are even functioning?"* *"How did you know how to be a husband?"* *A father?"* My healing comes from a complex process and encouraging community. It is found in a loving support system: my wife, friends, and new family; creating music as an outlet and through these scribbles that somehow made their way into a book. But most of all, healing comes from my faith in God. That's how I function, cherish my wife, and father my son.

So in response to questions I may ramble a bit, but my roundabout answers always end up speaking about the power of God's grace in my life. This God I was running from—the one I thought was so cheesy and too ridiculous to be real, turned out to be there. He was there offering grace at every turn. Now I know the truth: His loving hand held me the entire journey of my past, my present, and it continues to cover the shame from dark crimes and filth. That shame that bled from hurts too deep, so deep to the core it couldn't even break ground's surface. It is covered.

But here is some more truth—It's still not easy. Unfortunately, there were dark lies planted in me from my youth that still try to take root in my mind but I fight it with the truth. I also know I am a work in progress. I'm always growing, so I don't get discouraged as much when an ugly weed from the past tries to break through the soil.

Freaking Forgiveness (it's hard)
Another part of my transformation, and necessary process for my healing was learning forgiveness. I have forgiven mom for every situation she was either aware of or oblivious to. I wrote her in prison explaining all of this, but it was sent back to me without her ever seeing it, or knowing it was sent because I wrote it on the wrong kind of paper (yeah, that's a thing). She was released from prison on good behavior after serving 6 years and sometimes lives with Brother or Granny. My wife, my son and I have a love for her still to this day and hold no grudge against her. We

understand the harsh reality of mental illness, and even the side effects from drugs prescribed to treat the disease. Learning more about mental illnesses helped me in my forgiveness.

I learned in my journey too, that forgiveness doesn't mean I have to return to the way a relationship used to look. To stay healthy we set boundaries in our relationship with mom to resist falling into old patterns, to break cycles, and prevent reliving hurts. So, while we don't see her or visit with her in person, the love is real. There is love, a deep love from a son to a mother, but it looks different.

When I started to forgive mom I slowly (maybe even subconsciously) began to forgive myself. The expectations that I had and I felt others had for me began to fade. I realized the truth in my identity, in the way God the Father sees me.

"I am worthy and I am more valuable than gold"

A lifetime of feeling *less-than* was hardwired into my brain so any kind of truth is hard to believe. To give those words of worth life, I have to say them out loud. And repeat. And repeat again. I begin to see clearer. It's a long, slow process, but now when I get a compliment on my music, writings, or parenting I can start to accept it. Because when I felt worthless, no matter how many compliments were thrown my way (true or not) I would never believe it. I can see now that I am a good (enough) father. I am a good husband leading his family into truth. I always want to grow and be a better father. husband. loving human. But for now knowing I am "good enough" is more than good enough for me.

Where are they now?
We covered mom, but as far as my brothers and Granny go, I will randomly see them around or shoot them a text, but rarely keep close contact. However, me and Older Brother have grown closer the last few years.

Step-dad.
While I was writing all this down I realized that no matter how much of a goober I thought he was, Step-dad had kept us alive more times than not. Could he have been better? Probably so, but I'm still here, right? A few years ago I did some researching online, found out where he lived and his phone number so I rang him up. I think he was just as surprised to hear from me, as I was to be calling him. With a quiver in his voice from a recent stroke I could hear him crying as I thanked him for the times he was there to protect us. The conversation wasn't long but I knew the words held weight and there was a sense of closure. I found out two months after that call he passed away from cancer, so that final conversation means even more to me.

The Duprees.
The DuPree family I still consider my adopted family and see them at least a few times a week. DuPree Dad was actually a vital part in the design and printing of this book. The love they showed me as a teenager is something that gave me a real sense of belonging. If it wasn't for their acceptance, I'm sure this book would have a very different ending or maybe wouldn't even be a thing. Our relationship taught me that family is far more than blood and genetics. It's the people who love you, believe in you and encourage you when you think no one does. It's invites to *family-only* birthday parties, middle of the night hospital visits and prayer for mom's heart, 3 AM living room convos on life, love, and faith. It's a bond that reaches beyond the ordinary into the extraordinary. They taught me true family chooses you.

Dee's mom and dad.
Dee's mom and dad eventually saw the love for my bride was constant and unwavering and we all have become so close now. Her mom cannot even think about the way she treated me in the past without tears filling her eyes. Her dad has given us something even bigger than his blessing, his last name, which finally gave me a sense of belonging. Getting to carry on his name was his way of apologizing and going above and beyond in his efforts to show I am accepted. In doing so, I also pass this last name down to my son giving him that same sense of worth. It's a priceless gift to know he has a meaningful last name attached to a family that loves him with all their heart.

Brent.
Brent, the youth pastor from Linden who fed me hope like it was candy, is now one of my best friends and lives just a few miles away. He is still just as quirky and always quick to listen to anything I have to say. His influence in my life taught me that people are always listening, and watching. Now I think about the people I see on the daily and I'm more inclined to just love and care for them, knowing that actions and words really stick. He never once tried to shove the bible down my throat but instead just lived it out. I am thankful for his friendship and his truly caring heart.

Jessie.
Jessie is still one of the best "big sisters" a brother could ask for and a big part of our family's life. She is one of my wife's best friends and an aunt to my son. She is constantly calling or texting reminders that I am loved. We are similar in so many ways, so we can relate and hold each other accountable in our actions. Through this process I've learned so much about myself in the terms of how and why I react to situations. Sometimes I react out of the 'survivor-mode' of my past and it ends up doing more damage than if I would have thought it out. She gets this about me, so she is the one I call when I want to talk about those things. We push each other to make the right choice with our reactions. I love that we have the kind of relationship where we can be open and vulnerable about those situations.

The Roberts.
The Roberts still take our family in as their own once a year for vacation and so I can work on music with Danny. Their family has been a constant example of how I want to be as a husband and parent. Making music with Danny has been a huge catalyst for healing. When I can create something beautiful out of my pent up emotions, instead of pushing them back in, I am lighter. I am able to see things clearer and communicate through song when words will not do.

My wife + son + daughter
My wife. As far as the family I have grown in my own home, our bond is stronger than it's ever been and getting stronger at a steady pace. We go on nightwalks about 5 times a week when possible, and we constantly make music together. I still take her on dates and continue to pursue her to keep the magic. She is forever my best friend. This book process has taken my marriage to deep and sometimes dark places. But 15 years in, its depth feels like a bottomless wellspring reviving us with refreshing waters over and over again. That doesn't mean major arguments don't happen. Oh, they do. But instead of feeling worthless and shutting down in these situations I've learned to communicate. Getting through the uncomfortable conversations and letting my feelings out is so hard. But man, there is strength in those weak unguarded moments where our love for each other expands. We've discovered those vulnerable moments bring a closeness and intimacy that revive

and ultimately strengthen us. We have also learned in our journey together, in the difficult circumstances to grieve the disaster or lost expectation together (or separately), but we can't camp out there. For us, we must choose joy in spite of it all.

My son. Our relationship is the very picture of redeeming love. The unique way my son loves me gives me the confidence to be a good father. His sensitivity and empathetic heart show me that my role as a father has value. He's my best buddy. We finger-paint, watch Pixar movies, and drive around town with music blaring together for hours. We visit our favorite coffee shop and the baristas and regulars know he's following close beside me, but far enough from me so he has his independence. He can't tell me but he trusts me. It's in his eyes and the way he takes my hand when he knows we have to be attached for safety. Here lately he won't fall asleep until I have laid next to him in the dark for at least ½ an hour. From his room the other night as he fell asleep burrowed into my side I texted my wife, "What 13 year old boy wants to snuggle with his dad so he can fall asleep?" She replied, "One that has the father who has the Father's love in him and pours it out daily. One that God gave you specifically to redeem screwed up father stuff in your own experiences." Yeah, I'd say that's redemption.

My daughter. Over the past 4 years I have also gotten to father in a totally different way. We hosted a brilliant and generous boarding student from China, and what started just as a mentorship grew into something way more valuable. At first, it was simple. We had a spare room; she needed an American family while in the states—easy enough. As the time passed into years our whole family melded into something special. We were a real family. We still are. So many pictures of fatherhood were developed those years with Xiqing. I got to fulfill dreams of teaching my kid how to play guitar. Go on late night junk food runs for studying fuel. Send her off to prom looking like a princess after the girls took hours getting ready and taking pictures. Fathering her was a gift and total validation of what I had so desperately been looking for. I got to impart wisdom and truth and hear audible proof that my words were making an impact. She is in college now, sometimes in Cali other times in China, so we all still text, video chat and try see her any time we can. She's forever our daughter and one more reason I believe family is so much more than blood.

With an amazing core group of the perfect mix of friends and family, I am at a loss of words to express my thankfulness for the life I've been given.

So, as I look back on the paths I've taken and look forward to the roads that are yet to come, in both, I see the certainty and clarity of *hope*. It was always there and still is. This hope reveals that I am father, a husband, friend and a leader who has worth and a treasury of love. I'm not sure what happens next, but I am drowned in the clarity of what I have yet to see. So as the story ends, the rest of this journey just begins.

redemption of a father loving his son.

love and humor always bind us together

Afterword

So many people I would like to thank…

First off, I want to thank my wife, son and *forever daughter*. Thank you for making me a father and a husband and being a part of this whole journey. I love you with all my heart and there are no words to adequately portray how I feel about you.

To my mom for doing the best you could with what you were given and raising us boys mostly on your own. I know we didn't make it easy on you, and I'm thankful for the humor and great music taste you put in my ears as a kid. I hope you know the trueness of our love for you.

To my extra moms and dads I acquired over the years-Mama Kim, Boyd, Mama Crum, Papa Don, my sweet Mother-in-Love and Father-In-Law, Mama & Papa Roberts, Don & Kay Kay Balltzglier. Thank you all for filling a void. You have showed me how to be a father and a husband by your actions. The lessons I have learned from all of you are a life-changing gift that I will forever be grateful for.

To all of my friends who have become my sisters and brothers. There are way too many of you to mention individually and that in itself is a blessing. The love from all of you is an overflowing encouragement and reminder that Gods plan is real in my life. I don't know what life would be like and don't want to imagine it without any of you.

The design team Hanson Imageworks–Craig & Boyd, the way you believe in and champion me gives me the confidence that I can do this and I will forever be in your debt.

Kenny Rigsby your friendship and hard work you put into designing my website and branding timfrostspeaks.com is mind blowing. I am so honored to be your brother. Thank you for everything you do.

Rachel Mathew I know juggling one kid and being pregnant with another while tirelessly editing and proofreading this book was a chore. There are so many words of gratefulness I could offer for your sacrifice that would not do justice. I love you so much and couldn't have asked for a better editor.

Matt Hogan- the video you made captured our family perfectly. Thank you so much for your amazing talent and giving heart! Also, kudos for the video stills that made the inside and back cover.

Paul and Sara for last minute edits and awesomeness. We love y'all!

Dee None of the sleepless nights, working on book proposals, designs, printing pictures, worrying about the future, sweat, tears, and chair-falls, go unnoticed. There's absolutely no way I could have done any of this without you. So humbled and honored to be your husband. Thank you my love.

Lastly, I would like to address a centralized issue from this book that usually takes a back seat in our society—mental illness and special needs of all kinds. It's real easy to judge someone when his or her behavior or actions are different, extreme or make us uncomfortable.

Simply put, look past a condition and see the person. In our experience when people don't see our son as autistic first, but a human first…that's when all walls and pretenses fall. It's a balance like anything in life, right? Treat us like we are normal… but not so normal that any special needs or accommodations are ignored. He may seem oblivious to some eyes, but he is aware. He knows if he is seen as only a condition, and he will act out of that belief.

If you or someone close to you suffers from mental illness, dark thoughts or special needs seek help in the way of counselors, or reaching out to someone you trust. There is freedom in bringing your darkness to light, and healing in the release. Here are some sources you can check out.

National Suicide Prevention Helpline 1-800-273-TALK
And if you don't feel comfortable speaking out loud this is a helpful online chat room: http://www.crisischat.org

National Alliance on Mental Health
We love this organization and site because it's super readable and very informative. There are videos, current news articles and ways to help others with mental illnesses http://www.nami.org